The
Earth Chronicles
Expeditions

Also by Zecharia Sitchin

The 12th Planet
The Stairway to Heaven
The Wars of Gods and Men
The Lost Realms
When Time Began
The Cosmic Code
Genesis Revisited
Divine Encounters
The Lost Book of Enki

The
Earth Chronicles Expeditions

ZECHARIA SITCHIN

Bear & Company
Rochester, Vermont

Bear & Company
One Park Street
Rochester, Vermont 05767
www.InnerTraditions.com

Bear & Company is a division of Inner Traditions International

Library of Congress Cataloging-in-Publication Data
Sitchin, Zecharia.
   The earth chronicles expeditions / Zecharia Sitchin.
      p. cm.
   Includes bibliographical references and index.
   ISBN-13: 978-1-59143-076-6 (pbk.)
   ISBN-10: 1-59143-076-3 (pbk.)
   1. Sitchin, Zecharia. 2. Archaeologists—Biography. 3. Civilization, Ancient.
4. Civilization, Ancient—Extraterrestrial influences. I. Title.

CC115.S58A3 2007
930.1092—dc22
[B]

                                                          2007013884

Printed and bound in the United States by Lake Book Manufacturing

10 9 8 7 6 5 4 3

Text design and layout by Priscilla Baker
This book was typeset in Garamond, with Herculanum used as a display typeface

To my wife, who has traveled with me from the start
To my grandson Salo, and to Harvey and Kathie, who
accompanied me on special expeditions
And to the hundreds of inquisitive minds who went with me on
the Earth Chronicles Expeditions to see the past so that they
might understand the future.

Emblem of the Earth Chronicles Expeditions

CONTENTS

1

THE TROJAN HORSE

The first time I took a group of fans with me to Turkey, I made it a point to start that Earth Chronicles Expedition by going to Troy. Not because the site is the most interesting or impressive (which it is definitely not), and not because one can see there the remains of the famed Trojan Horse (which were never unearthed, now replaced by a wooden replica of how it had presumably looked—see plate 1); but because it is there that the notion of a Trojan Horse had originated—that of something that looks benign or benevolent, but that turns out to represent a hidden opposite surprise. Troy, in my scheme of the lessons to be drawn from visiting ancient sites, was my Trojan Horse.

The Trojan War is known primarily, but not only, from Homer's *Iliad* and *Odyssey*. It has been one of the most romanticized wars, known as the tale of the "love that launched a thousand ships"—the ships that sailed from Greece to the shores of Asia Minor to rescue and return the beautiful Helen, who had been abducted by a Trojan prince. Troy, under King Priam when the war broke out, was the principal and wealthiest of Greek settlements in Asia Minor, controlling much of the trade between Asia and Europe that lay just across a narrow strait. It was to Priam's dashing son, the prince Paris, that the goddess Aphrodite intended the beautiful Helen, daughter of Zeus, as a wife. But when Paris went to Greece to claim the prophecy's fulfillment, he discovered that Helen was already wed to Menelaus, king of Sparta. Helped by the absence of Menelaus, who was visiting Crete, Paris abducted Helen and took off with her and

Figure 1

a good deal of Sparta's treasure; persuaded that she too must accept the will of the gods, Helen married Paris in Troy.

When Menelaus returned to Sparta and discovered what had happened, he summoned all the Greek chieftains and called on them to help him recover Helen. They chose Agamemnon, king of Mycenae and the brother of Menelaus, as the expedition's leader. Outstanding among the Greek heroes (also called the Achaeans) was Achilles; on the side of Troy (also known as Ilion) a chief hero was Hector, the elder brother of Paris.

The heroes were guided (or sometimes goaded) by their varied gods or goddesses. The battles began with negotiations and then with a siege of Troy; they ranged over several years, with ups and downs for this or the other side, with lulls between battles, sometimes with single combat between the various heroes. Sometimes the besieged Trojans broke through the Greek ramparts and attacked the anchored fleet. Sometimes truces were declared for this or that purpose. Leading heroes got killed, on both sides. With both sides, but mostly the Achaeans, exhausted, the Greeks turned to a ruse as the final effort to win the war. With the help of the goddess Athena they built a wooden horse and hid their best fighters in it (fig. 1); then they burned their huts and boarded their ships, sailing away (but only to a nearby port). The Trojans, supposing that the war was over, were at first suspicious of the wooden horse, but in the end brought the horse into the city, an act that required pulling down part of the city's protective walls. At night the Greeks inside the horse stole out, attacked the Trojan guards, and lit a fire to signal to the Greek forces. The attacking Greeks spared no one, killing men, women, and children in the streets, in the houses. Menelaus reached Helen in her bedroom, where he

Figure 2

Figure 3

found her bedecked in lace. Her return to Sparta with Menelaus was the only happy end of the Trojan War.

The events of the war and what preceded it were described and romanticized by other Greek writers and poets besides Homer; the events were also recorded by paintings on vases or plates, mostly in classical Greek times (see fig. 2 and fig. 3). To the Greeks of antiquity, the events of the Trojan War and thus the existence of Troy itself were historical facts, never doubted. This becomes clear in the histories of Alexander the Great, who in the fourth century B.C. led an army of 15,000 men out of Greece to defeat the Persian armies and conquer the Asian lands all the way to India and to Egypt in Africa.

The histories of Alexander indicate that Troy was very much on his mind as he planned and carried out his campaign. They tell that a treasured possession of Alexander's was a copy of Homer's *Iliad*, given to him by his teacher, Aristotle. He chose to cross from Europe to Asia at the narrow straits of Hellespont (now called the Dardanelles—see map, fig. 4), a crossing point guarded a millennium earlier by Troy. Greek historians recorded that Alexander left the task of ferrying over his troops to one of his generals, while he himself took the helm of a galleon and steered it toward Troy. Once ashore, his first stop was at the temple of Athena in Troy; Athena was the patron goddess of Achilles, the hero most revered by Alexander.

The Persian armies were waiting for Alexander and his troops, and the first battle with them took place at the Garnicus River just northeast of Troy (in 334 B.C.). The puzzle of the Persians anticipating where Alexander would cross over could be explained by the fact—recorded by the Greek historian Herodotus—that the Persian king Xerxes, who had earlier invaded Greece, stopped at Troy on his way to Greece. There he climbed the remains of Troy's citadel, paid homage to its famed King Priam, and sacrificed 1,000 cattle to Athena at her temple. Since

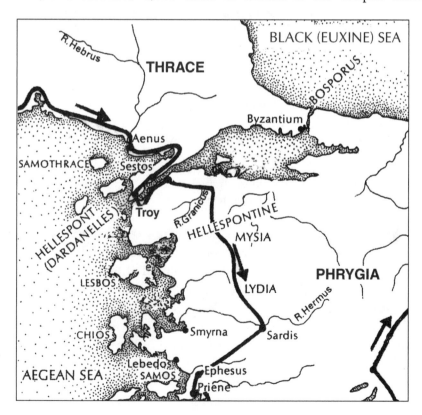

Figure 4

Alexander's infatuation with Troy, the *Iliad,* and Achilles was widely known, the Persian adversary of Alexander could well have assumed that the Macedonian would also come this way.

Roman historians and artists followed the traditions of their Greek predecessors in recollecting and depicting Troy and the Trojan War. Then, in time, the city and its war vanished from memory, literature, and art, to be forgotten for countless centuries. And when, by the Middle Ages, romances again chose the tale of Troy and its events as a favored subject, no one could tell anymore whether it was a true tale or just a work of ancient fiction. Where Troy itself had been located was also forgotten. So when medieval painters picked up the subject and depicted Troy and its heroes as soldiers in a city in western Europe in the fifteenth century A.D., it only reinforced the illusionary and unreal aspects of Troy and its tale. By the beginning of modern times, Troy had faded from the realm of history and emerged as belonging to the mythical past, no more a true tale than other fantastic tales such as the adventures of Odysseus, Jason's search for the Golden Fleece, or the Twelve Labors of Hercules.

The banishment of the story of Troy to rest among ancient myths was furthered in modern times by the fact that, when read carefully, the tale of the Trojan War emerges not as truly a War of Men but as a conflict initiated, controlled, manipulated, and participated in by the gods. According to the epic Greek tale *The Kypria:*

> There was a time when countless tribes of men encumbered the surface of the deep-bosomed Earth. And Zeus saw it, and having pity on them, resolved in his great wisdom to lighten Earth's burden. So he caused the great struggle of the war of Ilion (Troy) to that end, that through death he might make a void in the race of men.

With this purpose in mind, Zeus invited the Olympian gods and goddesses to a banquet, at which he caused a dispute between Hera, Athena, and Aphrodite as to who was the most beautiful of them. To resolve the dispute, Zeus suggested that the goddesses go to Asia Minor, where, near Mount Ida, Paris of Troy kept his flocks. Seeking his vote, each goddess offered him a reward if he chose her. Paris voted for Aphrodite, who promised him the love of the Fairest Woman in Greece; she turned out to be Helen, the wife of Menelaus of Sparta; and thus, the chain of events that led to the Trojan War began.

As the conflict erupted, gods and goddesses aided this or that side, provoked battles, lighted the skies at night to encourage continued battling, or snatched a favored hero from the jaws of death. The gods and goddesses, in time, took part themselves in the fighting, until Zeus ordered them to stop.

That the Trojan War was a tale of the gods rather than of men easily put the tale in the category of mythology. The fact that as archaeology advanced there seemed to be nowhere a trace of Troy compounded the classification. Troy, it was clear to all scholars, was just a myth.

***

It befell an adventurous businessman, Heinrich Schliemann (fig. 5), to dispel the myth and prove that Troy in fact existed. Born in Germany in 1822, he took a job in Amsterdam, mastered several languages, became a wealthy merchant in Russia, and took up archaeology as a serious hobby in Paris. After a divorce he married a Greek girl and moved to Athens; there Greek legends and myths began to guide his archaeological interests. Traveling extensively in the Hellenic zone, he accepted suggestions made by others that a site named Hissarlik at the tip of Asia Minor, on the eastern shores of the Straits of Dardanelles, was the location of ancient Troy.

Financing excavations with his own funds, he oversaw archaeological work at the site for almost two decades, beginning in 1870 until his death in 1890, when the work was continued by his assistant Wilhelm Dorpfeld. Schliemann's own excavations unearthed several successive levels of occupation at Troy, evidence of the city's fall at a time correlating with Homer's tale, and artifacts testifying to the city's opulence and period. A necklace, tiara, and other royal jewelry named King Priam's Treasure by Schliemann were gifted by him to his wife to wear in public (fig. 6).

Schliemann's discoveries at Troy, which he carefully documented and artfully publicized, did not result in the immediate appreciation that he expected. The scholarly establishment resented the intrusion into their realm by a self-appointed archaeologist. Few were ready to part with the notion that Homer's tale was just a myth. Accusations were made that Schliemann faked evidence, that some artifacts were really from other places. Even when, digging in Greece proper, he proved Homer right by uncovering ancient Mycenae and a royal tomb which he claimed was that of Agamemnon, he was still derided. A golden mask that he suggested was the death mask of Agamemnon was dismissed as a modern fake. And when his successor Dorpfeld (assisted and followed by other archaeologists) established that the site of Hissarlik was undoubtedly Troy, and that it arose from the third millennium in nine successive levels of occupation,

Figures 5 and 6

Schliemann's finds continued to be mocked because he thought that Homer's and Priam's Troy was at Level II, whereas archaeologists believed that the real Troy was at the later Level VII.

In spite of all that, many now consider Schliemann the Father of modern archaeology. Archaeologists now retain no doubt whatsoever that the site of Hissarlik is indeed the site of ancient Troy, and that in that respect *Homer's tale was no myth.* That Troy was destroyed, in the thirteenth century B.C. by siege and war, is also undisputed, though no one can say nowadays whether it was really about the beautiful Helen—or due to the wish of the god Zeus to lessen Earth's burden by getting some tribes of Mankind done away with.

Yet that is precisely why I chose to start the Expedition to Turkey with a visit to Troy; for, if Homer was right about there having been a city of Troy, and if Troy was in fact destroyed in a war, and if its treasures matched the Bronze Age period indicated by Homer, why doubt the rest of his tale—that not only men but also gods were involved in the conflict?

As the Expedition took the group to other exciting sites in Turkey, such as those of the Hittites or of Assyrian trading colonies, or to museums where artifacts from those past civilizations are kept, the reference to "gods" in inscribed texts and their depictions in countless monuments were omnipresent. As often as not, the depictions showed the gods as towering over their favored human kings. The gods are distinguished by

Figure 7

their horned helmets or other garments or footwear (fig. 7), or by the hieroglyph for "divine" or by the title "god" preceding their personal inscribed names.

To the ancient peoples, the "gods" were real, physically present. Without accepting that, traveling from one archaeological site or museum to another was, I felt, an exercise in futility. Having read my books, my group already knew that all the tales of gods hark back to the millennia-old Sumerian tales of the *Anunnaki,* "Those who from Heaven to Earth came."

***

To reach Troy from Istanbul one could travel via Turkey's main Asian part, passing several towns and cities in a densely populated part of the country, a journey by land of over two hundred miles. Or one could take the scenic (and in some respects historic) route on the European side, then cross the Dardanelles by ferryboat—as Alexander the Great had done (see map, page 5).

I opted for the latter, not only for its ancient links, but also because the route passed through the peninsula of Gallipoli, where Allied troops, in World War I, suffered tens of thousands of casualties in a failed attempt to quickly end the war by reaching the Turkish-Ottoman capital, Constantinople (now Istanbul), from behind the battle lines. After the war, the Turkish general who held off the Allied attacks adopted the name Ataturk ("Father of the Turks") and, deposing the sultans, led Turkey into the twentieth century as Kemal Ataturk, the first president and founder of modern Turkey.

The thirty-minute ferryboat ride, a pleasant and refreshing experience by itself, brought us to a small port town on the Asiatic side, where after a hearty lunch of locally caught fish we boarded our bus for about an hour's ride to the site of Troy.

One starts the tour of Troy's ruins by walking between the city's protective walls, whose lower and older courses, as in so many other ancient sites, are more massive and better fashioned than the stone blocks of the higher courses. The walk soon takes the visitor through excavations spread over a substantial area. The excavations are extensive, and at the same time haphazard-looking to the untrained eye: Troy has indeed been called in archaeological literature "the most excavated ancient site." The excavations cut vertically through at least seven levels of habitation ("occupation" in archaeology-speak) that start circa 3000 B.C.; it is only with the aid of the posted signs ("Level II," "Level Va," etc.) that a visitor can make sense of the remains of walls and buildings (see plate 2). It is when one stands at the highest point of the mound, from which the panorama of the surrounding plain can be viewed, that one can begin to gain a sense of history.

I climbed up to the topmost part of the ancient city and summoned the others in the group to join me. The sea has receded over the millennia, so no waters shimmered in the sunlight as they might have when Priam and his sons—perhaps from the same spot, the site of the ancient Upper City and its palace, where we now stood—looked upon the anchored Greek ships. The shoreline now lies some three miles away, adding perhaps to the expanse of the Plain of Troy where its river, the Scamender (Menderes in Turkish), still meanders. It was there that the angry gods tried to drown Achilles because the bodies of the Trojans he had slain clogged the river . . .

Turning to catch a 360-degree panorama, we could see in the southeast Mount Ida, where Zeus spent time watching and mocking the warring mortals. With the aid of binoculars one could glimpse, in the distant waters off the Turkish coast, the island of Bizcaada (Tenedos in Greek), from which the god Apollo came to the aid of the Trojans.

It is perhaps there, atop the ancient citadel, rather than when walking among the layers of ruins, that the tale of Troy as it was recorded comes to life in one's mind. Perhaps it is also the modern wooden horse (emulating earlier drawings, though clearly not an ancient relic) that somehow lends credibility to the place. It is located in the recreational area reached when one completes circling the ruins. In spite of its artificiality, the horse jolts the visitor and reminds one: Yes, this is Troy.

I felt that if Schliemann—a businessman turned archaeologist— proved that there was a Troy and a Trojan War, he also sustained the veracity of the rest of Homer's tale about the presence of the gods. The visit to Troy was thus a sort of Trojan Horse—a roundabout way to impress this sequential logic upon my traveling group.

2

THE CASE OF THE
HEADLESS SPACEMAN

This is a case of an almost Happy end:

After languishing in deliberate obscurity out of public view for almost a quarter of a century, a most unique and mind-boggling artifact was finally put on public display as a result of my persistence. Finally, I thought, anyone curious enough to resolve the enigma associated with the object could see and evaluate it for himself. And the enigma to be resolved was of great consequence: Was the artifact physical proof of ancient astronauts and spacecraft having been on our planet millennia ago—or was the object a clever forgery of recent provenance, and thus of no historic or scientific value?

I had every right to be pleased that the salvaging of the artifact from its intentional concealment and its placement on public display was a result of my personal endeavors. But the reader will soon find out why my victory was only an *almost* happy end.

First, let us look at the object itself (see plate 3). It is a sculpted scale model of what, to modern eyes, looks like a cone-nosed rocketship (fig. 8). It is 23 cm long, 9.5 cm high, and 8 cm wide (about 5.7, 3.8, and 3.5 inches respectively). It is powered by a cluster of four exhaust engines in the back surrounding a larger exhaust engine. And in its center, the rocketship has room for a sole pilot—a pilot who is actually shown and included in the sculpture.

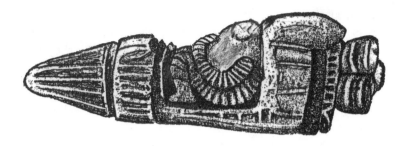

Figure 8

He sits with his legs bent up toward his chest. He wears a ribbed pressure suit; it is a one-piece suit that completely hugs the body. Down the legs and at the feet, it becomes bootlike. It extends and fully covers the folded arms, becoming glovelike where the hands are. The ribbed and presumably flexible suit encloses the whole torso—up to the pilot's neck (plate 3).

How did the suit continue thereafter? Did it become some kind of a head cover, did it stop at the neck with the head exposed, or did the pilot wear a separate helmet or some other kind of protective headgear? No one could know, because the pilot's head was broken off and was missing.

Did anyone know how the headpart came to be missing? Indeed, did anyone know anything certain about the object?

What I did know was that I had read, somewhere, that it had been discovered at an archaeological site in Turkey. I recalled seeing a drawing of it; someone in Turkey who had read some of my books had written to me about it. It was discovered in the region of Lake Van—the region where Mount Ararat (with its association to Noah's Ark) is located. If I were ever to visit Turkey, the letter said, I could see the object in the National Archaeological Museum in Ankara.

In 1990 my wife and I toured archaeological sites and museums in Turkey at the invitation of the Turkish government—as a result, it turned out, of the wife of the Turkish ambassador in Washington, an archaeology buff, having read my books. I seized the opportunity to inquire about the object, whose relevance to my writings seemed clear. When we reached Ankara, Turkey's capital, our reception was most cordial and lavish, and I was able to see and visit whatever I wished. But the object was not on display in the National Museum, and the Museum's director asserted that he had never seen, and certainly not held, such an object. If such an object does exist, he said, it would probably be kept in the Museum of the Ancient Orient in Istanbul.

Back in Istanbul, I and our host-guide paid a visit to the museum there. There was no such object on display, and in the absence of the museum's director, no one seemed to know anything about the mysterious artifact that, not having a photograph or a sketch with me, I could just vaguely describe.

Years passed. Then all of a sudden I came upon an item in the October/November 1993 issue of *Fortean Times,* a British periodical. Under the headline AN ANCIENT SPACE MODULE? there was a photograph which seemed familiar (see fig. 8, page 13) and the following short item:

> This object was excavated in the town of Toprakkale (known in ancient times as Tuspa). It is 22 cm long, 7.5 cm wide and 8 cm. high, with an estimated age of 3,000 years. To the modern eye, it appears to represent a space vehicle for one with the pilot's head missing.

The brief item then went on to state that "Some scientists have cast doubt on its age. It is kept in the Museum of Archaeology in Istanbul, but not exhibited."

The source of this intriguing news report was given as *Bilinmeyen,* vol. 3, p. 622. Although the British magazine put me in touch with its Turkish correspondent, the trail then went cold. The story, it seemed, was a revival of an old report, some ten years earlier, in a Turkish magazine that was no longer published.

As brief as the news item was, it contained several details that aroused my curiosity. There was, first of all, a photograph—meaning that such an object, enigmatic or not, actually existed. Its age (or antiquity) was stated: 3,000 years, which would make it circa 1000 B.C. And the place where it was discovered was given: the site of ancient Tushpa. I assumed that to the general reader of the British periodical the name of the site had little, if any, meaning. But I recalled (and later verified) that Tushpa was the ancient name of the capital of the kingdom of Urartu, known as Ararat from the Bible, on the shores of Lake Van; the twin peaks of Mount Ararat rise majestically right there (fig. 9).

In the first millennium B.C., Urartu was a major kingdom, a rival of Assyria to its south. At that time Urartian records employed the cuneiform script of Sumer and state documents were written in Akkadian. But the original language of the earlier settlers there was nei-

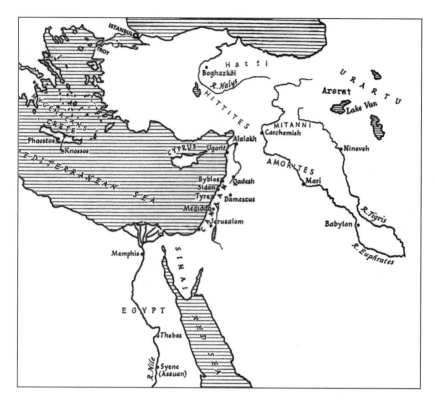

Figure 9

ther Semitic (as Akkadian was) nor Indo-European (as that of their neighbors to the west). Was it, perhaps, a precursor of Sumerian? Was the region of Ararat the early home of the Sumerians, who, according to the Bible, were people "who came from the east and settled in Shine'ar" (the Hebrew word for Sumer)? This, in fact, matched the Urartian lore and legends that they were descended from the survivors aboard Noah's ark.

But as interesting as all that was, my principal reason for curiosity as it related to the "Headless Spaceman," as I nicknamed the object, was indeed the space connection. As those who have read my book *The 12th Planet* know, the Sumerian texts concerning the Deluge (on which the Genesis tale was based) describe how the Anunnaki "gods," who circled the Earth in their air and shuttle craft during the avalanche of water, also landed on the peaks of Ararat. According to the Mesopotamian texts, the deity Enlil was enticed by the smell of the roasting meat when Noah made a burnt sacrifice to his gods.

To me, then, finding an ancient depiction of a spaceman and a rocketship at a place connected to the tales of the Deluge was thus not an outrageous impossibility.

But the most significant detail in the news report was this: the statement that the object was actually in the Istanbul Museum!

In March 1994, learning that the editor of *Magazin 2000,* Michael Hesemann of Düsseldorf, Germany, was going to Turkey, I asked him to use his press credentials to track down the artifact and its history. That he did, and published a report of his visit in issue no. 94 of his magazine.

Yes, it is here, he was told when he inquired about the artifact at the Istanbul Museum and showed a copy of the British article that I had sent him; and in less than five minutes the object was brought in! He was shown it, but not allowed to photograph it.

How and when did the object come into the Museum's possession? Hesemann asked. His printed report (translated from German) quotes the following answer:

> The object was confiscated a couple of years ago from a departing tourist. He acquired it and was going to take it abroad, although the export of antiquities from Turkey is illegal.

But why is this amazing artifact not on display? Hesemann asked. *Because it is a forgery,* was the answer! How can you be sure it is a forgery? the reporter continued to ask. Here is the answer he received, as quoted in the magazine:

> "It does not reflect the era's style, the era from which it supposedly comes. It looks like a space capsule—but of course there were no such things at that time. So someone has allowed himself a practical joke . . ."

In other words: It cannot be authentic because it would then authenticate something (astronauts, spacecraft) which could not be authentic. . . .

It was only when he was writing his report that it occurred to the German journalist to wonder: If the object was a forgery, of modern manufacture, why was it confiscated? Why was it not returned to the "tourist"?

The report in *Magazin 2000* prompted the editors of a competing German periodical, *GRAL,* to launch their own investigation. After several exchanges, they received in June 1994 a letter from the Museum, signed by Dr. Esin Eren, in which it was stated that the "object" was a forgery, made of "plaster of Paris and marble powder." But the letter gave an entirely different version of how the object came into the Museum's possession:

> The object was brought to the Istanbul Archaeological Museum in 1973 by a dealer in antiques, making it clear that he wanted to sell it. But when he realized that the object was a forgery, he did not ask to get it back. In the meantime, the encyclopedia called *The Unknowns* reported this object in its pages, leaking out this information. This is the source of the information given in the *Magazin 2000* of March 1994. The object in question is very light, due to the fact that it is a casting.

According to this version, then, there was no tourist and no confiscation. Rather, an unnamed antiques dealer tried to pull a fast one on the Museum, but abandoned the attempt when it was realized that the object was not authentic.

This version—an antique dealer whose name, address, and whereabouts were not known to the Museum—was repeated to two editors of *GRAL* when they visited the Museum later that year. Starting from the viewpoint that the object could not be authentic because only nuts believe in ancient spacemen, their conclusion was indeed that the object was a plaster-of-Paris cast of some modern toy. They could not find, however, any example of such a toy to compare with the object.

The conflicting versions of the artifact's origin, together with the initial denials of the Museum's awareness of it, only strengthened my curiosity—especially since I had reason to believe that the object could well be authentic.

Continually prompted by me, fans of mine in Turkey tried to find, and finally found, a copy of the *Bilinmeyen* magazine, issue no. 3. Bearing no date, but believed to have been published in the early 1980s, the report reproduced an entry in the *Encyclopedia of the Unknown* that had been published in Turkey in the 1970s in weekly installments.

Under the headline SCULPTURE OF SPACESHIP HIDDEN IN ISTANBUL ARCHAEOLOGICAL MUSEUM, the report stated that the artifact, whose picture was shown, was found ". . . during regular archaeological excavations in 1973 in the ancient city Tuspa (now known as Toprakkale) which is southeast of Lake Van, where the kingdom of Urartu flourished between 830 to 612 B.C. This extraordinary object is now in the Istanbul Archaeological Museum, but not on exhibit. The reason is not determined; there is no official statement about it."

Determined to pursue the enigma and unravel the mystery surrounding the artifact, I set the spring 1997 Earth Chronicles Expedition toward Turkey. Armed with a letter from the Turkish Embassy in Washington, I visited the Museum in Istanbul and met with the Director, Dr. Alpay Pasinli, and his colleagues. Pulling from my briefcase the various magazine reports and putting them on the Director's desk, I knew he would not be able to escape acknowledging that the object indeed existed somewhere in the Museum. "Why is it not on display?" I asked.

"We do not display forgeries," he said. Why was it considered a forgery? He gave two reasons: First, because there were no rocketships and spacemen in antiquity; and second, because no artifact is a unique and sole object—there is as a rule another find of a similar object, the same depiction, the same style, similar images—but this one is without comparison, so it is suspect to begin with, he said.

I disagreed with both points, but focused on his second reason. An object can be authentic even if it is a unique find, I argued; for example, the famed Phaestos Disc that was discovered in Crete in 1908 by reputable archaeologists. It is inscribed with hieroglyphic characters that

Figure 10

remain undeciphered because no similar object and no similar script have been found in Crete or elsewhere; yet the object is considered authentic beyond doubt (fig. 10).

Moreover, I pointed out, depictions of similar "rocketships" or their occupants have been found—perhaps not in Turkey, but certainly in the Americas!

"In the Americas?" he responded. "Can you show me?" When I return to New York, I replied; meanwhile, can I see the object? He hesitated. I must leave for a lunch appointment now, he said; come back at two o'clock.

He left, but I did not. "We are not leaving," I told my guide. "We will sit in the reception hall and wait." And we did . . .

After a long wait, the Museum's Deputy Director, Sefer Arapoglu, appeared. Dr. Pasinli called, he said; he is delayed. He asked me to show the object to you.

He led us to his nearby office. As soon as we entered, he went to a long cupboard and opened a drawer. From the drawer he took out a tray covered with dark blue velvet. A dark yellow, light brown object lay on the tray. "Here it is," he said, and held out the tray. "You can look, but no photos!" he added.

Thus, the three of us stood, and I had a first look at the artifact; it looked exactly as in the illustrations. But what now?

"Can I sit down?" I asked Mr. Arapoglu. Embarrassed, he said, "Yes, please sit down."

There was a coffee table and a small sofa near the windows. I went there and sat down. "Can I take a closer look?" I asked. "Could you put the tray down, on the table?"

He hesitated, but did as I asked. Reluctantly, he allowed me to turn the artifact over, then to hold it. Reluctantly he agreed that my guide could take a picture of it with my amateur's camera, providing I did not appear in the picture (but my hand does—see plate 4). As this awkward tug-of-war in which I tried to overcome this or that initial prohibition continued, Dr. Pasinli showed up, and we were all ushered into his office after the object had been hurriedly put back on its tray in the drawer.

"Well, what do you think?" Dr. Pasinli asked. "It looks like and feels like it was made of some porous material, some lightweight stone, but not plaster of Paris," I answered. I carefully checked it for casting marks, for the seam that results when the two cast halves are placed together and then removed; there was no such seam. The grooves that can be seen on the object are part of the craft's design. If it were a plaster-of-Paris cast, white material painted over outside, the white would be visible where the head had broken off; however, the yellow-brown color appears throughout—it is the natural color of the soft stone used.

Dr. Pasinli asked his deputy to bring in the object, and he then examined it to verify my observations. "Anything else?" he asked.

"Well," I added, "don't you notice a funny thing about the object? It is a flying machine without wings. . . . If a toy served as a model, it would emulate a winged airplane; even the space shuttle has some winged area. This one has none; so what was the model that served to show a rocketship with a single pilot?"

"So you say that it is a genuine artifact?" Dr. Pasinli asked.

"We both know," I said, "that without knowing when, where, and by whom the object, any archaeological object, was discovered, no one can vouch for its authenticity. It could be, after all, a fake. But who would fake a flying object the likes of which none have been seen in modern times, in reality or as toys? The object has been around since the 1970s; who had a plastic toy that served as a model at that time?"

At that moment, two gentlemen, dressed in suits and ties, came into the Director's office, and I thought it was a sign that I should leave. "No, wait," Dr. Pasinli said. "These gentlemen are from the Ministry of Antiquities. Please continue. . . ."

I repeated the points I had previously made. Then I added: "Unlike the previous time I was here, this time the Museum's old section, known as the Museum of the Ancient Orient, was closed because of lack of funds to keep it open (it was opened just for me and my group). So let me tell you this: If this object is not a forgery, you have in your possession something more significant than the Giza pyramids. Whereas the identity of the pyramids' builders is debatable—I and others say Extraterrestrials, others say pharaohs—you have incontrovertible evidence of spacecraft and spacemen in antiquity. So you have something unique! Thousands, tens of thousands of people would come to Istanbul, to the Museum, to see it. You think it's a forgery? Say so—but put it on display, let people judge for themselves! The admissions revenue would more than cover the cost of keeping the Old Museum open!"

The Director, his deputy, and the two officials from the Ministry of Antiquities exchanged glances. "Send to me the photos from the Americas, and we shall think it over," Dr. Pasinli said. "I certainly will!" I said as we left.

We took a taxi to the restaurant where my group had gone for lunch. It was hours past lunchtime, but they were all there. As I and the guide walked in, they fell silent, then someone cried out: Zecharia is smiling!

Indeed I was.

After I told them all that had taken place, we all agreed that the oddest part of the tale was that something deemed a worthless forgery by the Museum had nonetheless been kept for two decades in the deputy director's drawer on a velvet tray . . .

***

Back in New York, I airmailed to Dr. Pasinli the promised depictions, all illustrations from my various books. Some, like the one showing a rocketship in an underground silo in the Sinai (fig. 11), were intended to show him that manned flight was not an absurd notion in antiquity. Others were of depictions with similarities to the enigmatic object itself—primarily two stone tablets from Tula in Mexico (fig. 12), kept in the small museum there, which showed rocketlike craft akin to the one in Istanbul.

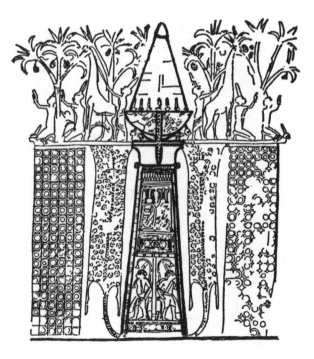

Figure 11

Figure 12

Figure 13

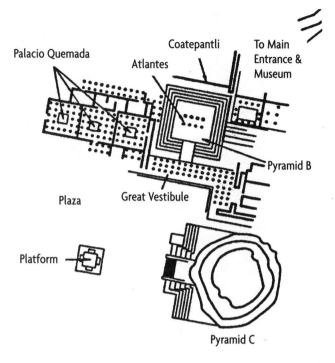

Figure 14

I attached particular significance to another depiction from Tula that showed someone attired almost exactly as the headless spaceman, but with the head and helmet intact (fig. 13). This one came from a carving on a stone column that visitors to Tula see but hardly notice (plate 5).

Tula was the capital of the Toltecs, who preceded the Aztecs in central Mexico. It was then known as Tollan ("the place of many neighborhoods"), and is believed to date back to about 200 B.C. Excavations showed that it had a sprawling religious-ceremonial center that included one large and two smaller pyramids (fig. 14). The few visitors that come there (including one of my groups on an Earth Chronicles Expedition) come mainly to see the *Atlantes*—fifteen-foot-high giants carved in stone (fig. 15)—"warriors" from another time (so presumed because they hold weaponlike tools), all dressed alike, but each with an individual face of an unknown race.

The stone giants, called *Atlantes* as a play on the legendary Atlantis, were found taken apart with their sections buried inside a trench in the pyramid called "B." The archaeologists restored them upon the pyramid's

Figure 15

flat top because it is assumed that the *Atlantes* served as caryatids, columns that support a roof. That this was so is indicated by straight four-sided stone columns, presumably serving the same function, found on the pyramid's top. These columns also bear carved images, but clearly of Toltec chieftains (fig. 16).

In 1985 I was visiting Mexico with my wife. We met with Gerardo Levet, an engineer who described in a booklet entitled "Mision Fatal" (Fateful Mission) a discovery he made at Tula/Tollan: On one of the square columns there is carved a depiction of a person wearing a protective suit and a backpack and holding a tool, akin to the "pistol" of the Atlantes, and using it as a flamethrower (fig. 17). He took us to the site to see the carving. His theory was that the pistol-like weapon held by the Atlantes, like the tool held by the person carved on the pillar, represented

Figure 16

Figure 17

Figure 18

a flamethrower, a kind of an Ultimate Weapon of the gods. But having seen in the site's museum the depictions on the stone tablets, I tended to believe that these were indeed flamethrowers; but *tools,* not weapons—tools used in mining operations.

The image in Tollan resurfaced in my mind soon after I saw the reports about the Turkish spaceman. The similarity between him and the small fellow in Mexico—especially if one adds a protective helmet to them (fig. 18)—was striking. All these depictions from Mexico tilted my opinion toward assuming the authenticity of the Istanbul object. I hoped, as I sent all the images to Dr. Pasinli, that he would also be swayed.

Several exchanges and reminders ensued. Then, in October 1997, I received a letter from Dr. Pasinli on the letterhead of the Istanbul Archaeological Museum. "I would like to inform you that the false space-rocket is finally displayed in our galleries," it said; "I expect you should be pleased now."

Yes, I was pleased, although the Museum had decided to mitigate the exhibiting of a "false object" by showing it together with other suspected archaeological forgeries, as the photo sent to me showed (plate 6).

So why did I start this tale by saying that it was a case of an *almost* happy end? Because, some time later, when a new Museum director replaced Dr. Pasinli, the object was removed from its display case. . . .

Where is it now? I believe it is back in the dark drawer resting on a velvet-covered tray.

3

ATLANTIS WITHOUT
SEARCHING

As fascinating as the legendary "Atlantis" has been, I have suc-
cessfully resisted the urge to join a very crowded field of
Searchers For Atlantis; but once, being in the proximity of one
of the many suggested sites of Atlantis, I said to myself (and to the group
that was with me), Let's take a look. When we had completed our inves-
tigations, not only did I find it possible that this legendary city once
existed, but we found intriguing evidence of transatlantic travel taking
place thousands of years ago.

If there is anyone who is totally ignorant of the subject of Atlantis,
let me tell it briefly: In two of his writings, the Athenian philosopher-
scientist Plato (428–348 B.C.) mentions "Atlantis" as an idyllic ancient
island-kingdom whose capital (or only city) was circular, with a central
harbor and dry land surrounded by other concentric harbors, all connected by canals. On the city's highest point there was a temple to the
God of the Seas, Poseidon; its enclosures and walls were covered with
gold. There was gold everywhere; the island was also blessed with copper
and tin. After a reign by Poseidon himself, ten of his sons inherited the
kingdom and divided it between them. The trade and influence of
Atlantis reached far and wide. Then, in one calamitous night, a catastrophe struck the city. A volcanic eruption of explosive proportions rocked

the island, blew it up, and caused everything to sink to the ocean's depths.

The information in Plato's dialogues *Timaeus* and *Critias* was, however, only hearsay. The source was an earlier philosopher-statesman named Solon, who was said to have reported that when he had visited Egypt, he heard the tale of Atlantis from Egyptian priests. They were reported to have said that it all happened at a time calculated to have occurred 9,000 years before Solon. Remnants of Atlantis's population who saved themselves by fleeing in ships brought civilization to Egypt.

Plato mentioned that Atlantis lay "beyond the pillars of Hercules," which means beyond the Straits of Gibraltar, where the Mediterranean connects to the Atlantic Ocean. Although this did not rule out the locating of Atlantis almost anywhere on Earth, it did establish the theory that it had been in the midst of the Atlantic Ocean as the prevalent theory, especially after the publication in 1882 of I. T. T. Donnelly's book, *Atlantis: the Antediluvian World.*

Twentieth-century researchers who scanned and verified the contours of the Mid-Atlantic Ridge, which runs at the ocean's bottom from north to south, have found, however, no spot that would fit the site of Atlantis. This to a large extent was the reason for shifting attention from the Atlantic and points beyond (the Americas, the Far East) and the 9500 B.C. date, closer to the source of the tale, to the Mediterranean Sea and the Greek islands.

Archaeologists established that the Minoan civilization that preceded the Mycenaean one in Greece developed on the island of Crete and blossomed on adjoining islands in the Bronze Age, but came to an abrupt end in the middle of the second millennium B.C. The builders of the Suez Canal in the 1860s used a volcanic material called pumice for cement and building blocks. It came from the island of Thera. It was not long before the evidence for a catastrophic volcanic explosion on Thera, causing earthquakes, tidal waves, and darkened skies, was linked to the sudden demise of the Minoan civilization. It was not much longer before Greek scholars connected Thera and its fate to Atlantis and its fate.

The Thera catastrophe, dated at first to 1250 B.C., attracted the interest of scholars in other fields, such as biblical scholars, for the eruption's aftereffects could be stretched all the way to Egypt to explain at least some of the calamities that, according to the Bible, befell Egypt prior to the Exodus (see map, fig. 19).

And so, in 1996, an Earth Chronicles Expedition to Greece and Crete was expanded to include the Greek island of Santorini, earlier

Figure 19

called Thera. After all, if not Atlantis, then the Exodus was definitely within the scope of my writings.

Getting to Santorini/Thera from the Greek mainland and from there to Crete could be done the leisurely way, by plying the seas aboard the weekly ferry. We chose to sail less and see more and took to the air in the small planes that shuttle back and forth—more frequently but less punctually (as one discovered). But in addition to saving time, we also got a bird's-eye view of the island.

Besides its official name, Santorini (after its patron saint, Saint Irene), the island was also called in the past Kallisti, meaning the Beautiful Island, and Strongulee, meaning the Circular Islands. Both names aptly describe the island for its beauty and its original true circular shape. Though today's island is only a remnant of what it had been, what remains clearly shows—whether from the air, from maps, from a mountaintop view or from a drive along the lagoon's perimeter—how the island once looked (fig. 20).

Figure 20

The volcanic eruption occurred off-center, to the island's west. The gap that the blowup left, a huge crater, is now a water-filled lagoon. The explosion left the eastern part of the island intact, to form the crescent-shaped main part of today's island. Of the western section there remains a narrowing rim of dry, mountainous land on which a most picturesque road has been paved. The rest of the western rim was reduced to two islands, one the small Therassia and the other the even tinier Aspronisi. The thinning rim plus the two islands complete the ring around the crater-lagoon, whose circumference is about forty miles.

A major tourist and scientific attraction on the main eastern part of the island are the remains of its local equivalent of a Pompeii: the excavated remains of a town named Akrotiri that was buried by the ash and pumice of the volcanic eruption. Visitors can now actually walk the unearthed streets of that town, view almost intact buildings, examine Bronze Age tools and artifacts (plate 7). Almost everywhere there remain standing, as on the day of the eruption, large storage jars. Here and there beautiful multicolored wall paintings survived the catastrophe; the style and the colors are virtually identical to those found on Crete, home of the Minoan civilization (fig. 21). Some of the murals, showing both passenger and cargo boats, attest to the island's maritime prowess (plate 8).

Since the calamity befell the island suddenly, one would expect to find among the buried dwellings and storehouses evidence of extraordi-

Figure 21

nary wealth, if Thera was indeed the Atlantis of Plato and Solon. But no such wealth has been found. The walls were painted with murals, but were not covered with gold (as the Atlantis legend held). There might have been some copper on the island, but no tin or other mineral wealth. The island, it is clear, was an offshoot of the Minoan civilization, not its center; would the great, rich, and powerful Atlantis be on the fringes and not at the center of the kingdom?

All the accumulated evidence, enhanced by the on-site visit, indicated that Thera/Santorini was not the legendary Atlantis.

Could its eruption be connected with the phenomena associated with the Exodus of the Israelites from Egypt? The answer depends to some extent on the datings. If both the Thera eruption (as some hold) and the Exodus (as many hold) occurred circa 1250 B.C., then a connecting argument could be made. If Thera's eruption occurred between 1500 and 1450 B.C. (as revised estimates indicate), a gap of two centuries occurs; however, if (as I believe) the Exodus took place circa 1450 B.C., maybe the two events coincided after all.

In my writings (and especially in *The Wars of Gods and Men*), by correlating biblical, Mesopotamian, and Egyptian chronologies, I concluded that the Exodus began in 1433 B.C., a date falling within only a few years from that arrived at by several other scholars. In 1986 Dr. Hans Goedicke of Johns Hopkins University caused quite a stir when he announced that a fresh reading of an Egyptian hieroglyphic inscription led him to conclude that the Exodus took place in 1477 B.C. (a date close enough to mine, as I stressed in correspondence with him). Moreover, he linked the crucial event of the parting of the waters of the Sea of Reeds and then the rush of waves that swallowed the pursuing Egyptians to the volcanic eruption in Thera and the immense tidal wave it had caused in the eastern Mediterranean.

As stated, other research regarding the Thera catastrophe before and after Dr. Goedicke's findings dated the eruption at between 1550 and 1450 B.C. With no other new discoveries, the Thera-as-Atlantis and Thera-as-Exodus-related theories went into hibernation.

∗∗∗

Was the visit to Thera unproductive, then, on both the Atlantis and the Exodus counts?

Not exactly. For the visit to Thera created a niche, if that is the right way to explain it, in my mind that was now labeled "Atlantis." And that led to a discovery on the next destination, the island of Crete.

The discovery neither proved nor disproved the existence of an island kingdom called Atlantis, but it left no doubt in my mind that sometime in the past—and we are talking about ancient yet historic times—people from the Old World found their way to the New World. Though the tale of Atlantis seemed to suggest that only Atlanteans had come east to the lands of the Mediterranean, it did not preclude journeys in the opposite direction, from the Mediterranean to the New World, the lands beyond the Pillars of Hercules. If so, then such travelers could bring back the reports of a golden city surrounded by waters. And if so, then Atlantis could have been reality, not myth or legend.

And that is what I could not avoid concluding on the island of Crete.

As tourists do, we chose to stay at one of the beautiful hotels in the island's capital, Heraklion, situated on the Mediterranean seashore. From there, as tourists do, we went to visit the ruins of Knossos, the ancient capital of Crete in Minoan times. The ruins are dominated by the excavated remains of the palace (fig. 22) of the island's famed king Minos

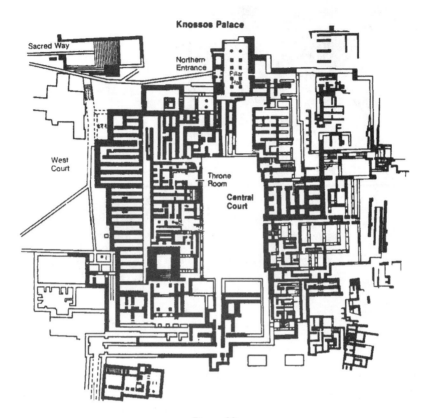

Figure 22

(thus the "Minoan" civilization), with which many of the legends of gods, demigods, men, and bull-men are associated. Much of the glory of Knossos saw again the light of day primarily due to the archaeological efforts of Sir Arthur Evans, mainly since 1900. He, and those who continued the archaeological excavations and the extensive reconstructions, uncovered palaces, storerooms, shrines, residential buildings, monumental columned structures, and a wealth of wall paintings in bright colors, spanning six centuries of Cretan life (fig. 23).

The next day, as fewer tourists do, we went to the Candia Museum in Heraklion, where most of the art treasures and artifacts discovered on the island are kept. While the official tour guide, as part of the routine museum tour, led the visitors to the displays of jewelry (to impress the female tourists?), I insisted on lingering at the less ostentatious displays, on tables protected with glass tops, of cylinder and other types of seals,

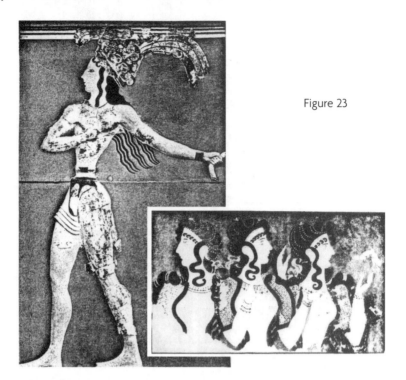

Figure 23

and other engraved objects. I was looking for a particular cylinder seal with an engraving showing what looks like a rocket in the skies above a procession of warriors, chariots, and fantastic beings (fig. 24). Although I had with me a copy of the illustration, and a clear indication that the seal was found in Crete and was at the museum, it was not on display among the artifacts there. Perhaps it's in Athens, I was told when I kept asking questions.

Figure 24

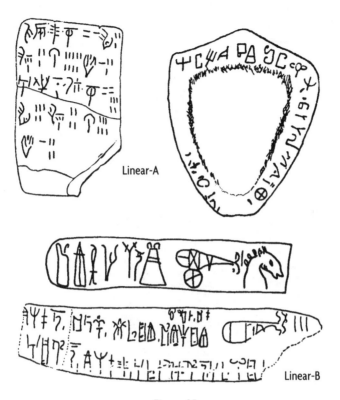

Linear-A

Linear-B

Figure 25

Disappointed that the seal was unavailable here, I shifted my attention to other important artifacts in the museum—the inscribed terracotta (baked clay) tablets with two similar but different scripts simply called Linear-A and Linear-B (fig. 25). Linear-B was more or less deciphered as a half-syllabic, half-alphabetical writing of the Achaean (early mainland Greece) people; Linear-A remains officially undeciphered although the late Professor Cyrus Gordon convincingly showed in the 1960s that it represented a Northwest-Semitic tongue, as from Phoenicia, for example. This would have conformed to the Cretan or Greek myths according to which Minoan civilization began on Crete when the great god Zeus saw Europa, the daughter of a king of Phoenicia, playing with her maidens by the sea. Taking a liking to her, he transformed himself into a bull and showed up on the beach. When Europa playfully climbed on the bull's back, he rose up and, swimming across the Mediterranean Sea, carried her off to the island of Crete. Once there, Zeus revealed himself to Europa and she agreed to mate with him; she bore him three sons, one of whom was

Minos, the famed Cretan king. Thus, this legend supports the suggestion that the earliest writing script on Crete emulated Phoenician-Semitic.

There was a third, and as yet mystifying, script found on Crete. It is the one inscribed on both sides of a terracotta disc known as the Phaestos Disc (fig. 26 and plate 9). It was discovered in 1908 in the ruins of a palace at the site called Phaestos on the island's southern shores. The archaeological context of the find dated it to the same period as Linear-A, 1700–1500 B.C.

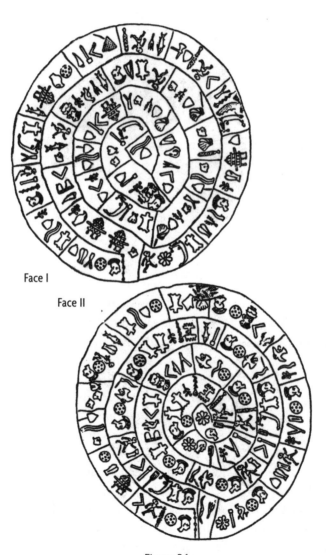

Face I

Face II

Figure 26

The inscription uses picture-signs—pictographs—written not by cutting the signs or glyphs into the palette, as scribes make them with a stylus or other "pen" when writing on wet clay; instead, the scribe of the Phaestos Disc used movable type to imprint into the wet clay—a type-setting method that was deemed invented by Johann Gutenberg 3,200 years later!

The pictographs of the Phaestos Disc, with a few exceptions, do not resemble any signs found in the two Cretan linear scripts. The 242 signs impressed on the disc's two sides were made from forty-five type stamps, which suggests to scholars that the writing was not alphabetic (fig. 27). Here and there a sign shows possible similarity to Egyptian hieroglyphs (which combined pictograms with syllabic signs), or to Hittite script signs. Because stamp seals (in which several words, or name and title, were preset to be impressed in wet clay, as on clay bricks) were used in Mesopotamia, some researchers sought the Disc's source and language in ancient Sumer. Without exception, scholars agree that the Disc was brought over to Crete from somewhere else. But from where, by whom, and what is its language?

Reviewing my briefing material before the tour began, one of the

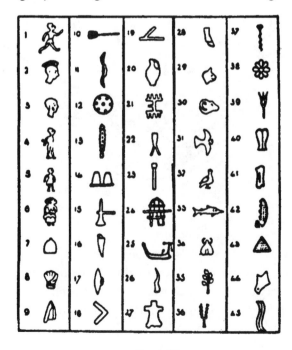

Figure 27

signs in particular had drawn my attention. As I looked closely at the Disc in its display case in Heraklion, I knew that I had indeed seen such a sign elsewhere. *It bespoke a link to ancient Egypt as well as to Chichén Itzá, the ancient Mayan metropolis in Mexico's Yucatán peninsula!*

The sign was that of a head, the head of a warrior wearing a plumed helmet. It is the most common sign after that of a man walking sign. It appears at the beginning of segments, as though it is the subject of the statement. Most of the time it is shown next to what looks like a shield; and, if the inscriptions begin at the bottom left (as shown in fig. 28), then the inscriptions on both faces of the Disc begin with this symbol, as though saying: This is the tale of the warriors who journeyed to . . .

Figure 28

The pictograph of a ship also appears on each of the Disc's faces several times, so a maritime expedition might well be recorded on the Disc. And that is where I first saw such warrior images before: in Egypt, on the temple walls in Medinet-Habu, on which the Pharaoh Ramses III recorded battle scenes with maritime invaders (fig. 29). The Egyptians called them "People of the Sea" and sometimes referred to them as Pelesht—a name virtually identical to the biblical name Plishti for the Philistines who had

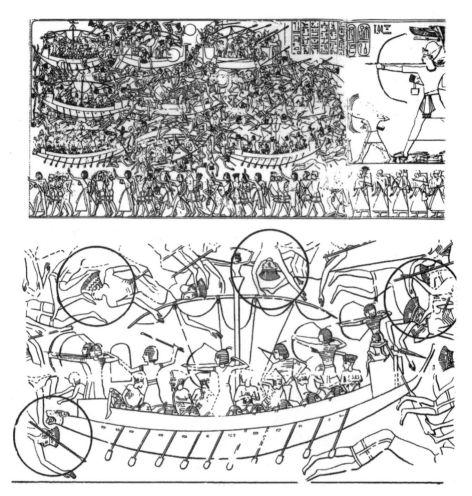

Figure 29

crossed the Mediterranean in boats to settle on the Mediterranean coast of Canaan.

The invaders' boats in the Egyptian depiction differ from Egyptian boats and are also virtually identical to the boat sign in the Disc. While the homeland of these invaders remains debatable, their depiction on the Phaestos Disc and Egyptian depictions from the thirteenth century B.C. leave no doubt that they were sailing the Mediterranean in the second millennium B.C.

That conclusion was the easy part; the next and more important question was: How far did those seafarers with plumed helmets go—did they go beyond the Pillars of Hercules, into the Atlantic? Did they sail as far as "Atlantis," bringing back news of its existence and its descriptions? My discovery of the very same warriors with plumed helmets at Chichén Itzá, on the other side of the world, provides an answer to these questions.

Chichén Itzá was a major Mayan center in the Yucatán peninsula of Mexico. It is believed that the settlement there began in the first millennium B.C. and that the place became the principal Mayan sacred city by 450 A.D. Its history, its monuments (the best known of which is the step pyramid, fig. 30), and its observatory are described in my book *The Lost Realms*. What is not mentioned in the book is that on one of my several visits to the site I decided to ignore the "NO ENTRY—PROHIBITED" sign and, maneuvering the wooden barricades that blocked the steps, I made my way up to a structure known as the Temple of the Jaguar.

Figure 30

The reason for my interest was the murals that were painted on the walls of this building. The ones on the ground floor that can be seen from the outside gave the building its name. But it was the murals on the upper (and blocked) floor that intrigued me, for sketches in textbooks seemed to show a scene of battle in which some of the warriors wore plumed helmets.

As I entered the upper floor and looked at the wall painting in its magnificent colors, I saw just what I had suspected. The mural depicted a fierce battle between Mayan warriors and invaders attacking a Mayan settlement (fig. 31). And there could be no doubt: The mural depicted the invading warriors as wearing plumed helmets. The similarity to the invading Sea Peoples in the Egyptian depictions and to the warrior sym-

Figure 31

bols on the Phaestos Disc was unmistakable. *Thus, the Disc was proof that the story of Atlantis could have indeed been brought back to the Mediterranean lands from across the seas.*

Who were those invaders, when and from where did they come?

According to the Mayan book of legendary history the *Popol Vuh*, and oral histories recorded by Spanish chroniclers after they reached the Yucatán peninsula, Mayan legends or recollections spoke of an invader or settler whom they called Votan. He was a leader of people from the Land of Can who arrived by boats on the coast of Yucatán from across the seas. His emblem was the serpent and he named the settlement he established Nachan, which means "the Place of Serpents." Some scholars see in the name Can a version of Canaan; Nachan is similar to the Hebrew Nachas, which also means serpent.

Chichén Itzá is located well inland in the Yucatán. Landfalls are believed to have taken place in the area of a site called Dzibilchaltun at the peninsula's northern edge, on the Gulf of Mexico. Archaeologists from Tulane University and *National Geographic* magazine dated the remains there to "between 2000 and 1000 B.C."; it is a date that matches the mid–second millennium B.C. of the Sea Peoples and the biblical Philistines.

For the tale of Atlantis, all this means that seafarers from the Mediterranean islands or lands in all probability journeyed—repeatedly (Votan made four voyages)—beyond the Pillars of Hercules as far as the Gulf of Mexico and Mesoamerica.

Now here is an intriguing thought: Was the pictographic writing on the Phaestos Disc the script of the Sea Peoples—or of the people of "Atlantis"? Since no other example of such a script has been found anywhere in the Mediterranean lands, logic suggests that it was a script from somewhere else. Could it then be that the seafarers from the Mediterranean, having reached a kingdom in the New World, not only returned with tales of it, but also brought, as physical evidence, a disc bearing a message in that kingdom's script?

And so it was that the visit to Thera, and then to Crete, opened my mind to the possibility of Atlantis. Like me, the ancient seafarers with the plumed helmets probably did not journey searching for Atlantis, but they could have come back to tell the Greeks and the Egyptians about it.

That such journeys in the recorded past have taken place became even more evident as I and my fellow travelers found, in Mesoamerica, that it had been visited by many other strangers from across the seas, as I will relate in the next chapter.

***

Postscript

The Phaestos Disc is still an unsolved enigma. Its uniqueness, as I have pointed out to the director of the Museum in Istanbul, attests to the fact that uniqueness, by itself, is no reason to question authenticity of an ancient find. The similarity of some of its symbols or pictographs to Egyptian depictions and *Mesoamerican* depictions of "Sea Peoples," as presented in this chapter, makes it merit much more study than it has received.

Thus, when the Expedition was in Crete, I suggested to the local tour operator that our program include a visit to Phaestos. His response was that it wasn't worth the effort; it was just a mini-Knossos and going there would entail a long drive.

"Well," I countered, "since I am in Crete and I am not sure if and when I'll be here again, I do want to see the place where the Disc was found." So Phaestos, a rarely visited archaeological site on Crete's southern coast, was included in the tour program. It was allotted one hour. The experts said that would be more than enough.

To say that Phaestos is a mini-Knossos is to be generous. There has been no restoration there, no remains of buildings with exquisite murals are still standing. You walk up the hill and see ruins, remains of stone structures, all around you (plate 10).

Our guide, Elena, was an archaeology major and quite knowledgeable. I asked her if she knew where, exactly, the Disc (called the Phaestos Disc simply because it was discovered in Phaestos) could be found. She said it was in the smelting area. She led us to the remains of a stone structure and pits.

"A smelting area?" I asked her. "This place was supposed to be, according to the guidebooks, a summer (or was it winter?) resort of the Minoan kings. This is very interesting," I said. "Was not Ephaestos, the god of smelting and refining, the Greek prototype of the Roman Vulcan? Does his name mean that he was from here, from Phaestos?" She replied that it might, although she had never heard this idea before.

I called the group together, telling them what I had just heard. If there was smelting and refining here, I told them, then this place was not just a royal resort, but an important industrial and commercial place, part of a complex chain of industrial and commercial centers in the Mediterranean involved in the production and trade of copper and bronze.

Let's spread out and see what we can find, I suggested. Look for the color green—it's a sign of the presence of copper. Look for conduits, where water was used in the manufacturing process. Look for anything that could be a clue!

We found green colorings and traces of copper ore (plate 11). We found water channels. We found artificial slopes that would have made it possible for the end product, large copper or bronze ingots, to be slid downhill towards the coast nearby. But no less, and perhaps more importantly, we found *writing*.

Here and there among the ruins my fans found a piece of ashlar (a hewn building stone) that had a sign engraved on it! Shifting our attention from the matter of copper, we launched an intensive search for signs of writing, checking one piece of stone after another. The search led us to a row of remains of stone structures that flanked what had to be a street. It looked as if the structures were merchants' stalls, since the rows of buildings seemed to have been subdivided into rectangular areas, each with its own entranceway.

There were signs—pictographs?—on some of the stones abutting some of the entranceways. We checked the insides of these "stalls." There was nothing but broken pieces of stone slabs, all covered with dust and soil.

"Can anyone spare water?" I asked. Someone stepped forward and offered her bottle of water. I poured the water on one stone to remove the soil and dust, and an inscribed sign came into view (fig. 32). We examined more stones, going from stall to stall. We were finding writing, the most important clue to deciphering the past, almost in every stall! Our guide said it was all news to her.

We took many pictures. We copied on paper as many signs as we could. We spent at Phaestos not the allotted one hour, but more than three. It was one of the most exciting aspects of the Expedition that I named "In the Footsteps of Mythology." We were not just seeing what others have found—we were actually discovering things on our own; we were not just studying archaeology, we were practicing archaeology!

We did away with plans to visit other places that day in southern Crete, and drove instead to a seaside restaurant, where they had expected us hours earlier, but still served us delicious seafood. Looking at the symbols we wrote on the pieces of paper, I observed that the symbols did not look like either Linear-A or Linear-B of the Cretan writing, and the guide concurred. "So what kind of writing is that?" I was asked.

I hesitated, then answered, "As unbelievable as it sounds, I can tell you that some of the signs look like early Sumerian pictographs." *Sumerian?!* was the response in unison. "Yes," I said; "it doesn't make sense, but that is what it looks like."

Back at the hotel, two members of the group undertook an assignment I gave them: Sort out the numerous signs we had copied and record each sign on a Sign Sheet. Lina J., a linguistics scientist with Intel, and Barry B., a computer expert, spent several hours doing just that. Then, at

Figure 32

that evening's briefing session, they presented their findings (fig. 33): There were twenty different symbols.

"Without my manuals I can tell you right off," I said, "that I see equivalents for Sumerian pictographs—the precursors of cuneiform— one for 'grain,' one for 'cloth,' and one for 'honey.' One sign is similar to that for a capacity measure, another for 'garment.' It looks like the merchant at each stall had inscribed on the entranceway or placed there a stone with a symbol telling what he was trading in!"

I promised the group that I would pursue this back home and keep them informed. Back in New York, my initial conclusions arrived at in Crete were confirmed. Moreover, it seemed that the precursor writing on

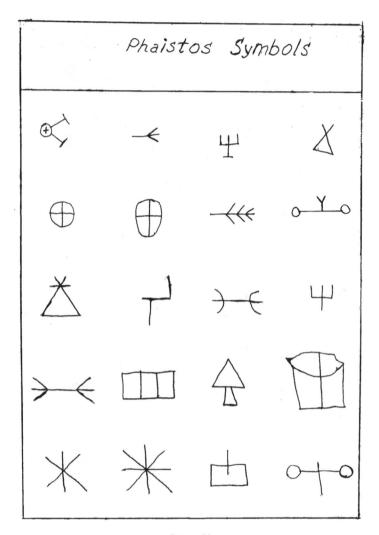

Figure 33

Crete, before the two linear scripts, was also pictorial and included some signs similar to the ones we found at Phaestos. I wrote about it to the Director of Antiquities in Crete, and to the American Schools of Archaeology in Athens.

No one bothered to respond. So I thought that I'd make our discoveries at Phaestos known via this Postscript.

4

STRANGERS IN
THE NEW WORLD

C an a stone calendar offer clues to the enigma of Atlantis? It might,
if it is a Mesoamerican relic; and if its carvings do not offer clear
cut solutions, it certainly adds new pieces to an expanding jigsaw
puzzle.

The National Museum of Anthropology in Mexico City, Mexico, is
undoubtedly one of the greatest museums of its kind—*national*. Unlike
the British Museum in London, or the Louvre in Paris, or the
Metropolitan Museum in New York City, that have assembled the cultural heritages of varied lands and peoples, a national museum is just
that—a museum dealing with the culture, art, history, and archaeology
of only its nation. Yet the archaeological treasures assembled in this
Museo Nacional in Mexico City include archaeological finds that, even if
not realized or intended by the museum's curators, serve as evidence of
unaccounted-for arrivals of Strangers in the New World at long-ago
times, long before Columbus, and provide reality to myths known only
on the other side of the world.

Built in a U-shape, the museum takes the visitor on a journey both
ethnological and chronological, starting from the earliest times where the
U begins in the right wing and ending with the more recent periods at
the opposite end. The center is dedicated to what the Mexicans consider
their particular heritage and link to Mesoamerica—the group of Mexica

Figure 34

(pronounced Meshicka) tribes that arrived in boats on the Pacific coast and wandered toward the land's central valley, where they found, as prophesied by legend, an eagle perched on a cactus plant, and thereby chose the site to build Tenochtitlán (The City of Tenoch), now Mexico City.

The pride and focal point of this principal section of the Museum is a great stone calendar that faces the visitor as one enters (see fig. 34 and plate 12). A similar one, but one made of pure gold, was the most sacred object kept in the Aztec's main temple and was presented by the Aztec king Montezuma to Hernán Cortés in 1519, when the arrival of Cortés was deemed by the Aztecs to be the fulfillment of prophecies of the Returning God. (Cortés sent the sacred object to Spain to be melted for its gold, and the Aztecs paid dearly for treating him as a savior.)

What has remained is the stone calendar, and it has been studied, analyzed, described, and interpreted without end (including in my book *The Lost Realms*). It is presumed to depict the Five Ages into which

Mesoamerican lore and legend divide the history of mankind and its gods. Each of the four previous ages ends with or by some calamity (including a great flood), and the fifth is the Age of the Mexicans and the Earth's other peoples, the current time.

I have been to Mexico countless times, and whenever I am in Mexico City I go to this magnificent museum (and know it so well that when some object is removed, I would notice it at once). I have stood and gazed at the great stone calendar numerous times.

And each time I wondered: Why is the central figure, that of the god of the Fifth Age, sticking his tongue out?

The textbooks and guidebooks, when they do explain, say that the depiction is that of Xolotl, "the god who fell from heaven," who is always depicted with his tongue sticking out (fig. 35). Mesoamerican legends relate that, appearing from the skies, he fell down or landed in a field, giving rise at that place to the two-stemmed maize (corn) that is the staple food of Mesoamerica.

Figure 35

But why does he stick his tongue out, that being his distinguishing feature?

To that I have found no answer in the textbooks dealing with Mesoamerica. Instead, I did find an answer all the way back in the Old World—in the Mediterranean lands.

It was when I was boning up on Greek mythology in preparation for an Earth Chronicles Expedition to Greece and Crete in 1996 when I first paid attention to depictions that I had seen but not noticed before of the

Figure 36

Gorgons (fig. 36). They were three sisters of divine or semi-divine ances-try who were once very beautiful but were changed into monstrous and hideous creatures by the goddess Athena. They were depicted with ser-pentine hair, glaring eyes, and a protruding tongue. In fact, the protrud-ing tongue was always the distinguishing detail even when the depictions differed from place to place and from one period to another.

According to Greek myths, the three Gorgons were daughters of a sister-brother couple of sea gods (Phorcys and Ceto). The daughters' names were Stheno (meaning "Strength"), Eurayle ("Wide Leaping"), and Meduza ("Reigning Queen"). All three were very beautiful, but espe-cially so was Meduza. Attracted by her beauty, the great god Poseidon, Lord of the Seas and brother of Zeus, came to make love to Meduza; and of all places, he chose to do so in a temple dedicated to the goddess Athena.

Furious, Athena placed a curse on the Gorgons and turned their beauty to ugliness. She also persuaded Perseus, a demigod, to go and kill Meduza. It was a dangerous assignment, for Meduza acquired a magical power to turn whoever set eyes on her into stone. Armed by Athena and other gods with magical implements of his own, Perseus used Winged Shoes to fly to Meduza's abode "in the distant west, beyond the Pillars of Hercules." Flying over Africa and reaching the great ocean, he followed "the Ocean Stream." He found Meduza and her sisters asleep in "the Rain Forest." Wearing the Cap of Invisibility, he managed to approach Meduza. Using a bronze mirror to see her without looking at her (fig. 37), he cut off her head with a unique sword that a god had made for

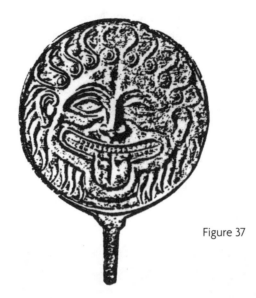

Figure 37

him; then he placed the severed head in a special pouch and flew away. The two other Gorgons, who were awakened by the happenings, could not see him because he wore the Cap of Invisibility.

The geographic clues contained in the tale are reinforced by the rest of the myth's story. Flying eastward over the great ocean, Perseus was quite tired and barely made it to the shore of North Africa, the home of Atlas. But Atlas was inhospitable, so Perseus turned him into a stone mountain by showing him the severed head of Meduza. Then, continuing eastward over Libya, Egypt, and Philistia, Perseus at last returned to Greece; there he founded Mycenae, where Greece's mainland civilization began.

The geographic details in the Tale of the Gorgons cannot be dismissed as mere fantasies of a myth teller. The abode of the Gorgons is described as a "rain forest," a tropical or semi-tropical area, "in the distant west" across a great ocean, beyond the Pillars of Hercules; a place that could be found by following the "ocean stream"—an excellent way of describing the Gulf Stream, which flows, as an ocean river, from the Gulf of Mexico across the Atlantic Ocean to the English Channel. Once cooled in the seas of northwestern Europe, and assisted by the Trade Winds, the current returns to the Caribbean and Mesoamerica by a more circuitous route.

Though flying, Perseus, according to these tales, followed a circuitous route that was familiar to seafarers even in antiquity, a route also followed by Columbus in his voyages from the Mediterranean to the Caribbean in the New World. The geographic clues, along with the distinctive detail of the protruding tongue, indicated a strong link between the Greek Gorgons and the central deity in the Aztec calendar.

But the Gorgons were females, and the deity in the Aztec calendar appears to be male. Could it be that somehow, at some time, the female-male distinction faded away and only the protruding tongue remained as the lasting connection?

Until 1995 scholars classified depictions of the Gorgons into nine types, some of them losing their femininity and assuming more masculine features (fig. 38). But in 1995, archaeologists discovered two large sculptures of Gorgon heads at Tell Dor, an ancient seaport on the

Figure 38

Figure 39

Mediterranean coast of Israel south of Haifa. Of one of the heads only fragments were found; the other one was quite intact—and it definitely looked like a representation of a male "Gorgon" (fig. 39). Other artifacts discovered at the site suggested that Tell Dor had close trade and cultural links with Mycenae in the late Bronze Age (1500 to 1200 B.C.) and was settled after that by Phoenicians and Sea Peoples from Cyprus, Crete, and other islands and lands in the eastern Mediterranean. The Tell Dor Gorgon head—displayed with other intriguing artifacts in the Maritime Museum in Haifa—is dated to the sixth and fifth centuries B.C. It offers both a confirmation of a transition to Gorgon male representations and physical proof that confirms the legendary clues about direct contacts in early times between the Mediterranean and Mesoamerica.

These were not the only clues, as a closer look at what is in the museums proved.

✳✳✳

The great Aztec stone calendar is full of details, each undoubtedly there for a reason. Many have tried to understand the depictions of the Ages and read calendrical meanings in their designs; some have found prophetic indications too. I, accepting the basic depiction of the past four Ages (because texts and oral lore also spoke of them) and the fifth and current one, have avoided such speculations; the stuck-out tongue and its links to the Mediterranean seemed intriguing enough for me.

But, as I was to find out later than sooner, there was even more in the calendar's designs related to that specific subject of linkage to the Old World.

A detail in the stone carving, at the bottom of its outer ring, looks from a cursory view to be merely decorative curves. I must admit that I, too, no matter how many times I have looked at the carved stone or its depictions, have failed to notice right away that what is carved there is not a decoration, but the *faces of two men,* identical, except that one faces right and the other faces left, toward one another. And what is most significant is that the two are *bearded* (fig. 40).

In *The Lost Realms* I dwelt at length on the puzzle of "the bearded ones" whose depictions are found throughout Mexico in Toltec, Mayan, and Olmec sites (fig. 41). The point of puzzlement is not only that the racial types so depicted are not Olmec or Mayan or any other American-Indian, but that American-Indians have no facial hair; they are never shown bearded because they never grow beards. So the Bearded Ones, as I have nicknamed them, had to come from another place on Earth. To judge by their racial features, that other place was the Mediterranean (fig. 42).

Figure 40

Figure 41

Figure 42

In the course of examining bearded Mediterranean types, it seemed significant that the principal gods of the Greeks, both Zeus and his brother Poseidon, were bearded (Zeus, fig. 43; Poseidon, fig. 44). Moreover, their beards seemed very much like the beards worn by some of the men in the Mesoamerican depictions (see fig. 41). Was it possible then, I wondered, that the Bearded Ones on the stone calendar depicted not men but gods?

Such a line of thinking brought me back to Greek mythology, with emphasis on the principal deities, the bearded Zeus and Poseidon. While Zeus was the head of the pantheon of the twelve Olympians, he shared control of Earth by recognizing the seas as the domain of his brother Poseidon. In that, the Greek pantheon clearly emulated the Sumerian one, with Zeus emulating Enlil, the Sumerian "Lord of the Command," and Poseidon comparable to the Sumerian Ea ("Whose Name Is Water"; later known as Enki).

The parallels between Poseidon and Ea/Enki went beyond the genealogy and hierarchical divisions. According to Greek myths, Poseidon was quite promiscuous, and in making love to Meduza had sex with a female

Figure 43

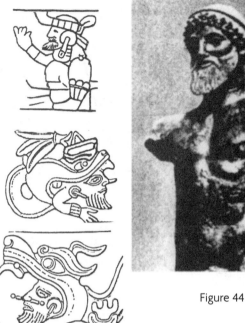

Figure 44

of his own family. Sumerian tales recounted similar escapades for Ea/Enki. Besides being the god of seas and flowing waters (fig. 45), Ea/Enki was hailed as a great scientist and the one who employed genetic engineering to bring about *Homo sapiens*. Accordingly, his symbol is that of Entwined Serpents, representing the double-helixed DNA. The same symbol was

Figure 45

"Ptah"

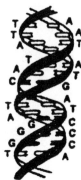

Figure 46

the hieroglyph for his name, PTAH, in Egyptian (fig. 46). This might explain the puzzling fact that the Gorgons were sometimes depicted with entwined serpents (fig. 47).

Poseidon, through the tale of the Gorgons, emerges as a principal motivator of the events beyond the Pillars of Hercules. Likewise, one must recall, does he emerge as the principal god of Atlantis. Is the depiction of two bearded entities at the bottom of the Aztec calendar meant to be a mirrored image of him, or of him together with his brother Zeus?

Figure 47

Were the bearded Sea Peoples, beholden to their god of the seas, the ones who journeyed to and from Atlantis, abode of the Gorgons?

In more ways than one, the Aztec stone calendar—a document of history more than of mere timekeeping—seems to record ancient links between the Old and New Worlds. All this seems to suggest that "Atlantis"—the legend or the reality—was in the Americas; and to narrow it down: in Mesoamerica.

Roaming the exhibit hall's section about the Mexica, one comes upon a depiction, as an imagined bird's-eye view, of the Aztec capital, Tenochtitlán, as it looked when the Spaniards arrived (fig. 48). It was a kind of Mesoamerican Venice, an island surrounded by a lake and a city dissected and ringed by a series of canals, with a sacred precinct and a major temple in the center. When the Spaniards arrived they were struck and amazed by the city's thriving commerce, the traffic of boats, the opulent and colorful vestments, the riches expressed in golden objects.

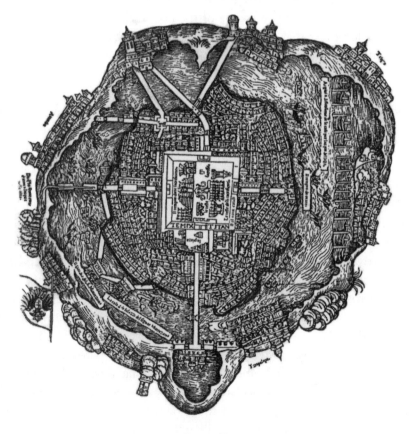

Figure 48

As I stood by the exhibit, my mind began to wonder: Were the Spaniards seeing, in Tenochtitlán, a replica of Plato's Atlantis?

I still wonder.

***

The connecting threads between the Old World and the New World, between both peoples and gods, go well beyond what I have discussed so far.

On my first trip to the Yucatán peninsula, accompanied by my grandson Salo, I came upon certain artifacts that could justifiably be called amazing; I shared those findings with the groups that joined me later on the Earth Chronicles Expeditions.

The first discovery concerns a (then) obscure museum in Yucatán's principal city, Merida, and it has to do with Enki, when he was still Ea, and the Sumerian tale of his arrival on Earth at the head of a group of fifty astronauts. The main source of the tale is Ea/Enki's own autobiography, a long text that, regrettably, was found damaged and with many gaps (and that was used by me to reconstruct *The Lost Book of Enki*). The text describes how Ea's pioneering astronauts, coming from their planet Nibiru, splashed down in the waters of the Persian Gulf, waded ashore, and erected shelters—the first alien settlement on Earth, which they called Eridu ("Home in the Faraway").

In the third century B.C., after the death of Alexander the Great, the Seleucids (his successors in the Levant, the lands of the eastern Mediterranean) commissioned a Babylonian priest, Berossus, to write down for them the histories and pre-history of the world, of men and gods, as recorded in Mesopotamia (Chaldea to the Greeks). His writings, known only from fragments copied by subsequent historians, begin with that arrival on Earth by Ea, followed by the creation of Man and the granting of civilization to Mankind. As the later Greek historians retold what Berossus had written, Ea became Oannes, a god dressed as a fish who came out of the waters and waded ashore and gave knowledge to Mankind.

On my first visit to the Yucatán peninsula and its Mayan sites, my grandson and I stayed in Merida, a Spanish colonial town with no archaeological attributes. It was by chance that I heard that a collection of artifacts discovered in the peninsula could be seen in a private villa turned into a museum. Though not yet fully open to the public, we were let in.

The whole exhibit was set up on the first floor (much more was in the basement, I was told). The director of the museum, whom I had persuaded to let us in, showed us around. His pride was a collection of samples of advanced dentistry by the Mayas. My attention was drawn, however, to a carving on a stone that showed a "star" accompanied by the Mayan Eight symbol (fig. 49a). It's from a temple in Chichén Itzá, the director said; it is associated with the planet Venus.

I could not hide my excitement: The rayed "star" was exactly how the Sumerians depicted planets (fig. 49b). Moreover, they considered Venus, the planet of the goddess Ishtar, to be the eighth planet of the solar system, and frequently depicted Ishtar with an eight-pointed star (fig. 49c)

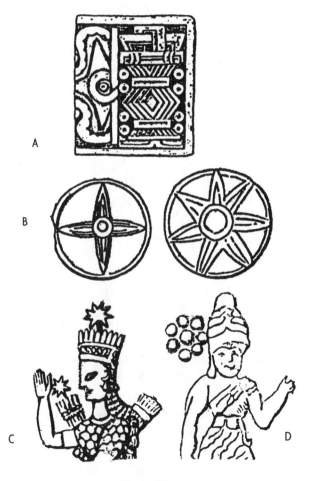

Figure 49

or accompanied by the symbol of eight circles (fig. 49d). Incredibly, in all these details the Mayan depiction matched the Sumerian ones!

Through a doorless doorway I glimpsed a sculpture—a rather large block of stone the front of which was sculpted to portray a male image (fig. 50 and plate 13); under his right arm he was holding a symbol of a rayed star!

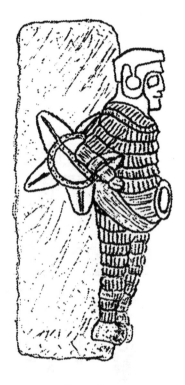

Figure 50

With quick steps I approached the oddly carved statue. Only the front part of the large stone block was sculpted, while the back half of the sculpture remained an uncarved stone block. The man was depicted with strong facial features, certainly not Mayan. A helmet protected his head but did not hide his face. He was shown wearing a full-body ribbed suit with a texture that had the look of fish scales. The suit covered his whole body, from the neck down to his feet; but the feet were either left unsculpted or were sculpted so as to leave unclear what his footwear was. An enigmatic circular device was attached to his belly, held in place by two belts; it reminded me of a headlight.

"What is *that?*" I asked the museum director. "It's a Water God," he informed me.

"It's Oannes!" I shouted out to my grandson and to the bewildered museum director.

I then had to explain, to tell the tale of Ea's arrival, splashdown, wading ashore, what Berossus wrote, and so on. But what is such a depiction doing here, in the Yucatán, rather than in Mesopotamia? I wondered.

The museum director said the carving was discovered in the northwestern part of the Yucatán. Other large sculptures were also discovered at a place called Oxkintok; archaeologists presume they were carved pillars erected to support the roof of a temple. All kinds of odd sculptures were found in the Yucatán's northwestern corner and nearby islands, he said with a smile; one of them, Dzibilchaltun, is where the famed Seven Dolls were found . . .

I took several photographs of the enigmatic sculpture and studied them later at home. One intriguing aspect of the sculpture was the question of how many rays the star had, for the man's arm hid some of them. It could have been just five, or it could have been six. If six, it could denote Mars, the sixth planet as the Anunnaki entered our solar system, counting Pluto, Neptune, and Uranus as the first, second, and third planets they encountered; Saturn and Jupiter as the fourth and fifth; Mars as the sixth; Earth as the seventh; and Venus the eighth. If it was a six-pointed star, depicting Mars, the statue in Merida could be linked to a depiction on a cylinder seal from Mesopotamia, dated to circa 2500 B.C., and now kept at the Hermitage Museum in St. Petersburg, Russia. The seal shows an astronaut wearing a fish suit on Mars and one wearing an eagle suit on Earth, with a spacecraft in the heavens between them (fig. 51). Mars is

Figure 51

depicted as a six-pointed star; Earth is designated by the seven dots, and its companion, the Moon crescent, is seen nearby.

It is all very intriguing, very mysterious. Who was the sculptor? Who or what was the model? The questions remain unanswered, but the connection of this stranger to Sumer and its tales stands undisputed.

***

As the reader might well guess, we could not leave the Yucatán without going to Dzibilchaltun, the site mentioned by the director of the museum in Merida. At the time it was a place which few people, if any, visited; since then I have taken a few groups there, and the authorities have developed the site's paths and improved its small museum. To locals and visitors it is known as the place of the Temple of the Seven Dolls.

The site is one of the largest—or more precisely, the most elongated—of the Mayan sites in the Yucatán. A raised walkway, well over a mile long, runs from one end to another, with various structures built along the way. The principal temple at the northern end, built as a step pyramid with a tower, is so constructed that when someone (an astronomer, a priest?) stands on a platform some distance before the temple, one can see the sun rise on the day of the equinox, its rays shining through the tower's openings. It was there, in the tower, that the seven dolls which gave the temple its name were found.

I asked the local guide where the seven dolls were, expecting some sizable statues. He took me to the site's museum. "There they are," he said.

On a stand, seven small dolls were placed in a circle. I looked puzzled. "That's it?" I asked. "That's it," he replied.

So what was so special about a few small dolls?

As I looked closely—and as the photograph shows (plate 14)—they looked like tiny *astronauts with backpacks*—similar, I recalled, to the photographs that showed a U.S. astronaut stepping off the Landing Module on the Moon (fig. 52).

Who fashioned these dolls, who were his models, why seven?

I wish the dolls could speak.

***

Figure 52

Postscript

Alerted by the Seven Dolls of Dzibilchaltun, I asked participants in sub-sequent Expeditions to Mexico to be on the lookout for depictions of such beings with astronaut-like backpacks. Among the memorable ones discovered was a small sculpture of an "angel," equipped with feathered wings and a protruding backpack, exhibited in the entrance museum at Chichén Itzá (plate 15), and a petroglyph (rock carving) exhibited in the Early Mexico section of Mexico City's great museum that depicts a giant-like being with a distinct backpack (plate 16).

These were startling finds; they suggest a much more widespread awareness in ancient Mesoamerica of beings who could roam the skies.

5

THE ELEPHANT AND
THE ASTRONAUT

In 1869, farmers in Mexico made an unusual discovery. The embarrassment that it caused evidently continues to this day. My tale of it includes two museum visits, a missing elephant, and a "leap of faith" by an American astronaut.

The ruins and remains of Mexico's pre-Colombian civilizations enchant, intrigue, and fascinate. One of them is also embarrassing to some: It is the oldest and earliest, that of a people referred to as Olmecs. It is an embarrassing enigma, because it challenges scholars and prideful nationalists to explain how people from *Africa* could have come to the New World not hundreds but *thousands* of years before Columbus, and how they could have developed, seemingly overnight, the Mother Civilization of Mesoamerica. To acknowledge the Olmecs and their civilization as the Mother Civilization of Mesoamerica means to acknowledge that they preceded that of the Mayans and Aztecs, whose heritage the Spaniards tried to eradicate and Mexicans today are proud of.

We know that the Olmecs were Africans because we know how they looked. We know how they looked because they left behind countless stone carvings and sculptures that depict them. Some are portraits-in-stone of their leaders, including colossal stone heads.

The first of quite a number of such colossal stone heads was discovered by farmers in the Mexican state of Veracruz in 1869. A report of the discovery described it as "a work of art, a magnificent sculpture that most amazingly represents an Ethiopian." Accompanying drawings reproduced the head's Negroid features and a sketch showed the stone head's great size in comparison to a man standing near it.

The sculpture, unique as it was with its disturbing features, was soon ignored and allowed to be forgotten. It was not until 1925 that a second gigantic head (it measured about eight feet in height and weighed some twenty-four tons) was found, this time in the adjoining state of Tabasco by an archaeological team from Tulane University. The find indicated that the first stone head discovered was not merely an unusual aberration in Mexican archaeology. In time, many more such colossal stone heads have been discovered. Comparing them to each other clearly shows that they are portraits of different individuals, all wearing helmets which were not always identical (fig. 53). It was also clear that they were all black Africans.

As archaeological discovery followed archaeological discovery, it became evident that the "Olmecs" first settled on the Gulf coast of Mexico,

Figure 53

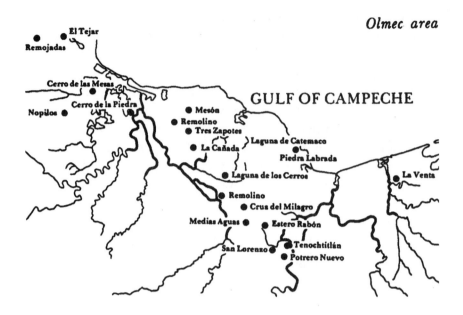

Olmec area

Figure 54

spreading inland and in time reaching Mexico's Pacific coast (see map, fig. 54). More than twenty Olmec sites have been uncovered, some bearing by now famous names such as La Venta, Tres Zapotes, San Lorenzo, Cerro de la Piedras. I have gone with my expedition groups to the most significant Olmec sites. The first time I went on my own (accompanied only by my grandson Salo) it was to see the major Olmec finds from La Venta, which had been transferred to the city of Villahermosa and set up there in a park museum to protect them from damage by oil drillers.

The colossal stone heads were the prime attraction, and their size can be judged by one of the photographs (plate 17). But size was not the only or most impressive aspect; what impressed me most was the artistry and craftsmanship of these sculptures. And not just the heads—throughout the park museum there were placed great slabs of stone whose faces were carved with the most complex details—some showing Olmec parents holding their children (fig. 55), or showing them with elaborate headgear (fig. 56). It seemed certain to me that in some if not most instances, the headgear and tools held by the depicted Olmecs were associated with mining.

Figure 55

Figure 56

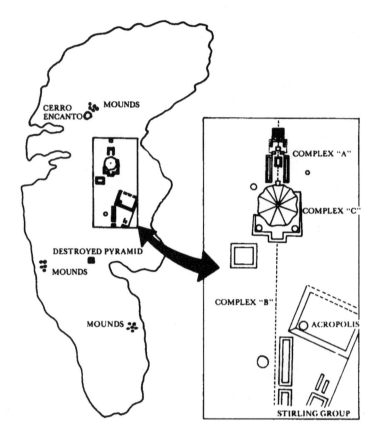

Figure 57

The archaeological discoveries left no doubt that the Olmecs built complex urban centers—some, as at La Venta, with pyramidical structures of great size and with astronomical alignments (fig. 57). The Olmecs engaged in mining, attained high levels of art, introduced hieroglyphic writing to Mesoamerica, and were also the first in Mesoamerica to have a calendar. They were, in other words, both the first and the Mother Civilization in Mesoamerica.

The enigma of the Olmecs presented a double puzzle: How could black Africans cross the Atlantic Ocean long before Columbus? And how long ago did it happen?

The Olmec enigma was dealt with at first by suggesting the least oldest date for their origin: 250 B.C., which would put them into a latecomers category. But as one Olmec site after another was dug up, the date kept shifting back to 500 B.C., then even 1250 B.C. Since my own date for the arrival of the Olmecs in Mesoamerica (a date coupled with an explanation of the circumstances of their arrival) was 3100 B.C., I was pleased to read in the official guidebook of the La Venta Park Museum a slight concession. It dated the Olmecs' first settlement on the coast of the Gulf of Mexico to "between 1350 and 1250 B.C.," and elsewhere in the guidebook to an even earlier time, conceding "the appearance of the first civilization of Mesoamerica a little under 4,000 years ago"—i.e., around 2000 B.C.

But the older the Olmec civilization became, the more did the problem become one of national pride. Unable to deny the existence of the Olmecs and also their antiquity, Mexican anthropologists began to assert that the very notion of Africans crossing the Atlantic millennia ago was baseless—because (they said) the so-called Olmecs were indigenous people, Mesoamericans whose features just happened to have a resemblance to Africans.

Such an inventive way to explain away the enigma of Olmec origins is clearly expressed in the official catalogue of the best museum in Mexico dedicated to the Olmecs, the Anthropological Museum of the University of Veracruz in Jalapa (sometimes spelled Xalapa). The introduction, written by a noted Mexican scholar, states in regard to the persons depicted in the Olmec sculptures that "in spite of the general similarity of features—flat noses with flaring nostrils and thickened lips (leading some to falsely claim an African origin for the Olmecs)," they were indigenous people and not strangers from across the seas.

And such statements that the suggestion of African origins for the Olmecs is a false claim bring me to *The Case of the Missing Elephant.*

Jalapa, a gem of a town situated in the cooler mountains about two hours' drive from the hot and humid Veracruz (where Hernán Cortés landed in 1519), now boasts a new museum that is second in excellence only to the National Museum of Anthropology in Mexico City. But unlike Mexico City's museum, which displays artifacts from all over the country, the one in Jalapa exhibits only locally discovered artifacts—predominantly Olmec ones.

The museum dramatically and effectively displays, in an innovative setting, a wealth of artifacts from the Olmec period, including several colossal stone heads. One of them is displayed right at the entrance, which serves as an inviting spot to take one's picture; other stone heads are displayed among trees and greenery in open courtyards, placing them in a more natural surrounding (plate 18).

Also displayed are smaller objects associated with daily Olmec life. Among them, in special display showcases, are toys. They include animals on wheels—yes, *wheels,* which, according to accepted scientific notions, were unused and unknown in the Americas at that time (plate 19). And included among the toys are (or I should say *were*) toy elephants made of clay (see plate 20).

I and my fans visited the Jalapa Museum for the first time on the Earth Chronicles Expedition in April 1995. The significance of the toy elephant was immediately obvious: There are no elephants in Mesoamerica; indeed there are no elephants anywhere in the New World. So, for anyone (Olmecs, in this case) to make for his children a toy elephant he had to have seen an elephant before, somewhere else. The toy's maker could have seen elephants either in Africa or in Asia; given the distinctive racial features on the Olmec sculptures, the place had to be Africa.

Back in the hotel that evening, giving my daily Briefing Session, I compared the finding of the toy elephant to the climax scene in the movie *Planet of the Apes,* which tells the story of astronauts from Earth returning home after a life-suspending space journey, only to find the planet inhabited and run by intelligent apes. Their suspicions that the place was their home planet Earth but that somehow humans had been replaced by apes are finally and dramatically confirmed when they find a rag doll of a human girl in a cave on the beach. "This elephant toy is our equivalent of the human rag doll," I told my group. "This is incontrovertible evidence that the Olmecs not only looked like black Africans, but that they actually came from Africa, a place of elephants."

In December 1999 I was again in Jalapa, specifically to visit the museum there. Losing little time, I led the group that accompanied me to the section where the smaller objects, including the toys, were exhibited. I told the group of the elephant found there last time, and the cameras were ready.

But there was no toy elephant. It was no longer there—gone, vanished!

Museum employees who were questioned at first claimed to have no idea what I was talking about. But when the empty space was pointed out, someone suggested that the item was away "on loan" to another museum.

That was hard to believe, because of something else that was missing in the museum.

***

I could call it *The Case of the Missing Date Column;* it has to do with dating the arrival of the Olmecs in Mesoamerica.

While establishment archaeologists have conceded dates ranging back to 1500 B.C., based on examination of excavated strata, I looked at the problem from a totally different angle. One of the achievements of the Olmecs was the introduction to Mesoamerica of the oldest of its three calendars. Mesoamericans utilized a Sacred Calendar of 260 days, called Tzolkin; a practical calendar, Haab, of 365 days; and the Long Count calendar, which began from some enigmatic Day One and kept dating events or monuments by counting how many days had passed since that Day One (fig. 58). The Long Count calendar was the Olmec contribution, and scholars have been able to establish that Day One coincided with August 13, 3113 B.C.

To me it seemed to make sense to begin the calendar from a date that held great significance for the Olmecs, just as the Western common calendar uses B.C. to denote "Before Christ" and A.D. for "Anno Domini," years since the birth of Jesus. So what was the Olmecs' significant event? Could it be, I asked myself, the date of their arrival in Mesoamerica, or the arrival of the great Mesoamerican god Quetzalcoatl ("The Winged Serpent")?

The Mesoamericans believed that Quetzalcoatl promised to return when the "bundle" of the two other calendars, the cyclical ones, meshed and returned to a common starting point. That happened once every fifty-two years (including the year 1519 A.D., which is why the Aztecs welcomed Cortés as the Returning God). That number seemed familiar to me: It was the Sacred Number of the Egyptian god Thoth—the keeper of divine secrets, a divine architect, giver of calendars.

The story of Thoth in Egyptian mythology, related in my books *The Stairway to Heaven* and *The Lost Realms,* was dominated by his rivalry with his brother Ra. The Egyptian historian-priest Manetho, who was first to list Egypt's rulers by dynasties, recorded a time when Thoth reigned over Egypt, a time when demigods beholden to him reigned, and a time when he was exiled from Egypt by Ra. It was then that Pharaonic reign—Egyptian civilization—began. This is universally dated to circa 3100 B.C. So the thought occurred to me: Could a more precise 3113 B.C. be the date when Thoth, exiled from Egypt, arrived in Mesoamerica with a group of African followers (Egypt, let us recall, is in Africa)?

Such a solution to the enigma of Day One fitted well with the

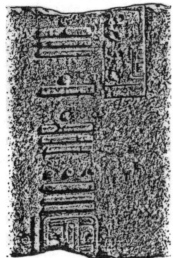

A. The Long Count: the number of days since August 13, 3113 B.C.

B. Tzolkin: Sacred Year of 20 x 13 days

C. Haab: Solar Year of 365 days; 18 months of 20 days + 5 "nameless days"

The Sacred Round: The interlocking of B and C into a grand cycle returning to the same position every 52 years, as when Cortés arrived in 1519 A.D.

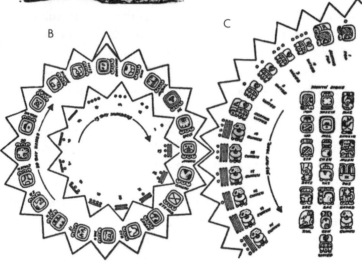

Figure 58

significance of 52 in the Mesoamerican calendars. So, if I was right, this date—circa 3100 B.C.—was when the Olmec civilization began.

Imagine now my thrilled astonishment, as I entered the Jalapa Museum for the first time, to see that a whole wall to the left of the entrance was covered with a mural depicting Mexico's varied cultures in a chronological sequence. The longest column was the first column, denoting the Olmecs. Its antiquity reached all the way down, almost to the floor. As I studied it, I could not believe my eyes: The date indicated for the start of the Olmec civilization was *3000 B.C.!*

I shouted to my group to come at once. "Look at that! Look at that!" I shouted with uncontrollable exhilaration: "3000 B.C.!"

"Take a picture! Take a picture!" I called out to my fans. And they did (plate 21). I had been vindicated!

So, this time in 1999, marching with my fans once again into the Jalapa Museum, I led them to the chronological wall, even before they had a chance to settle for photographs near the Olmec head. And then it was my turn for a second disbelief: The whole Olmec column, the first column in the chronology of cultures, was gone. Deleted.

Luckily, there were in the group some who had been there with me on the first visit, and they swore with me that there had been an Olmec column showing 3000 B.C. To make sure my fans continued to believe in my integrity, I promised to send each one a copy of the earlier photograph, which I did.

The disappearance of the column led me to doubt whether the Missing Elephant was just loaned to another museum or was deliberately made to disappear. Letters to the Museum inquiring about it have all remained unanswered.

***

Do I then have only that photograph, showing me pointing down to the 3000 B.C. date, as the only proof of the tale of Jalapa and the date of Olmec beginnings?

I thought so until the U.S. astronaut Gordon Cooper published his memoirs a year later, in 2000. Titled *Leap of Faith*, its publisher subtitled the work "An Astronaut's Journey into the Unknown," and stated on the dust jacket that in the book, Cooper (one of the original Mercury Seven astronauts) "takes dead aim at the next millennium of space travel with his strong views on the existence of extraterrestrial intelligence—and even the distinct possibility that we have already had contact."

Based on that description, I bought a copy of the book with a certainty that I would find in it an astronaut's revelations on what he and his colleagues saw while in space, or what NASA knows, revelations that have a direct bearing on the Anunnaki and Mankind's contacts with Extraterrestrials. Instead, I was at first disappointed, and then elated to find out that Gordon Cooper's "leap of faith" had nothing to do with NASA secrets, but stemmed from his coming upon Olmec ruins.

"During my final years with NASA," the astronaut wrote, "I became involved in a different kind of adventure: undersea treasure hunting in Mexico." One day, accompanied by a *National Geographic* photographer, his small plane was forced to land on an island in the Gulf of Mexico. Seeing them, local residents led the Americans to ancient pyramid-shaped mounds, which they thought the visitors had come to see. There the visitors found ruins, artifacts, and bones. On examination back in Texas, the artifacts were determined to be 5,000 years old!

"When we learned of the age of the artifacts," Cooper writes in a chapter titled "Stumbling Upon History," "we realized that what we'd found had nothing to do with seventeenth-century Spain. . . . I contacted the Mexican government and was put in touch with the head of the national archaeology department, Pablo Bush Romero." Together with Mexican archaeologists, they went back to the site. This is what transpired (page 188):

> Together we went back to the ruins, which the government knew nothing about. The Mexican government ended up putting some funding into the archaeological dig. *The age of the ruins was confirmed: 3000 B.C.*

The civilization to which the ruins belonged, the archaeologists told him, was that of the relatively little-known *Olmecs*.

Considered the mother culture of civilization in Mesoamerica, Cooper explains (page 189), the Olmecs were credited with developing writing in Mexico, and had introduced the concept of Zero and positional numbers, a great agriculture, and great public buildings. As skilled engineers, the Olmecs managed to transport huge blocks of basalt and other stone from quarries more than fifty miles away from their sculpted monuments. "A lot of hieroglyphics were found at our site," Cooper wrote, and "the sculpture found at the site was divided between representations of supernatural beings and of humanoids." Continuing, he wrote:

> Among the findings that intrigued me the most: celestial navigation symbols and formulas that, when translated, turned out to be mathematical formulas used to this day for navigation, and accurate drawings of constellations, some of which would not be officially "discovered" until the age of modern telescopes.

It was this, rather than his experiences as an astronaut, that triggered Gordon Cooper's Leap of Faith (page 190):

This left me wondering: Why have celestial navigation signs if they weren't navigating celestially? Did this advanced navigational knowledge develop independently in three different places in the ancient world at the very same time? If not, then how did it get from Egypt to Crete to Mexico? And if so, reason dictates they must have had help. If they did have help, from whom?

I could have not put it better myself. I wrote Gordon Cooper to thank him for corroborating my dating of the Olmecs to 3000 B.C.

***

This tale, too, has a postscript.

On the 23rd of January 2001, Gordon Cooper and I were guests together (via long-distance phones) on the popular nighttime radio program "Coast-to-Coast AM." The host, Mike Siegel, asked the former astronaut to tell the audience about the finds off the coast of Mexico, and he did. I explained the significance of the dating of 5,000 years, and asked Mr. Cooper to reaffirm that, and he did. Whatever happened to the finds? I asked. They were taken to Mexico City, he said. Was there a follow-up, did he hear more about the discoveries? No, he said. Could he try to find out? Yes, he said, he would try.

Fans of mine recorded the interview, of which I have a copy.

If anyone visiting the museum in Jalapa should rediscover there the elephant toy, or find the Olmec date column reinstated, or, on visiting the museum in Mexico City come upon the finds from Cooper's island—please let me know. Meanwhile, I will not be holding my breath.

6

THE GODDESS WHO
ROAMED THE SKIES

I wanted to visit Mari ever since I had seen the goddess.

    I saw her, or more correctly a picture of her, for the first time when I came upon a group photograph of the French archaeologists who, in the 1930s, were excavating the ancient site of Mari on the Euphrates River. I knew from their reports that they were all males; so I was astonished to see them clustered around a good-looking female, as one would

Figure 59

stand around a visiting dignitary (fig. 59). Odd, I thought; it required a second look, after a pause for incredulity, to realize that the female was a *statue*—so lifelike and lifesize she was.

Mari, it was known from deciphered Sumerian King Lists, was the tenth rotating capital of the political-religious entity known as Sumer & Akkad, which blossomed out in Mesopotamia (see map, fig. 60). Royal archives of inscribed clay tablets indicated that Mari grew from a boat-building and river-crossing place at the end of the fourth millennium B.C. to a major center of international trade in the third millennium B.C. There was a hiatus, a dark period, for more than a century around 2000 B.C., and then it served as the tenth and last capital of Sumer & Akkad, from about 1900 B.C. until it was overrun and destroyed by the Babylonian king Hammurabi in 1761 B.C. Then its fame and glory faded into oblivion, its remains were covered by windblown sand, and it was completely forgotten.

As in so many other instances, it was a chance discovery of some protruding remains by passing nomads that led archaeologists to be summoned. Excavating for six years until the outbreak of World War II in 1939, French archaeologists (under André Parrot) unearthed the remains of a major capital whose main palace was the largest ever found in the

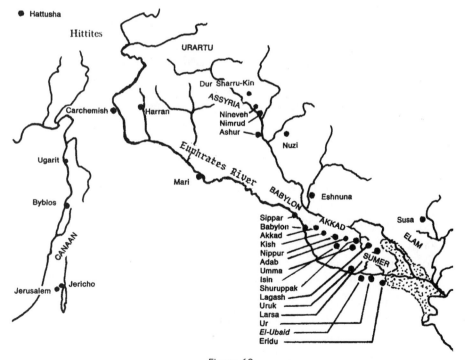

Figure 60

Figure 61

ancient Near East. Statues of kings and governors, exhibiting an artistry that matched that of classical Greece but dating back to more than a thousand years before Greece, bore their names in the clearest cuneiform script (fig. 61). More than 20,000 (yes, 20,000) inscribed clay tablets from royal archives clearly indicated that this was the lost city of Mari, and bore evidence of the extent of its economic, political, and military reach along the Euphrates River and beyond. Royal correspondence with the mighty Assyria to the northeast, with Bedouin chieftains in the south, and with such city-states as Ebla in the northwest (a place whose remains and archives were found only decades after the discovery of Mari) attested

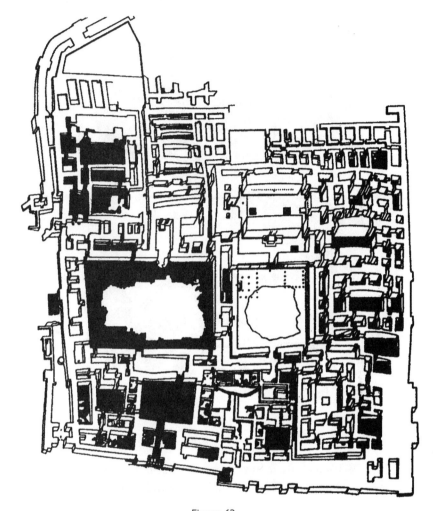

Figure 62

to the standing of Mari in the nineteenth and eighteenth centuries B.C.

What was found among the buried ruins matched in opulence and grandeur the attestations of the royal exchanges. The main palace consisted of more than three hundred rooms built over an area of five acres (fig. 62). There was a stage-temple (ziggurat) and multiple-halled temples; the whole royal-sacred precinct was surrounded by walls in which gates had been installed that opened and closed in a most ingenious and modern-looking way (fig. 63).

In the palace, in the temples, and in special scribal rooms there were

Figure 63

records. Everywhere there were statues, statuettes, cylinder seals, and other artistic depictions of Mari's deities, as well as of its dignitaries, soldiers, citizens, merchants, and peasants (fig. 64). They all bore witness to

Figure 64

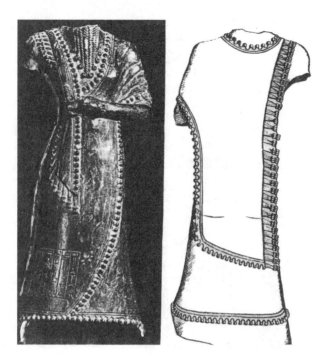

Figure 65

a highly developed civilization and a wealth that could support art and elegance (fig. 65).

Of particular importance, both historical and cultural, have been the magnificent colored wall paintings—murals painted on a layer of white plaster spread on the clay brick walls, mainly but not only in the great palace. Framed by images of flowing waters and palm trees, the murals depicted scenes of gods and kings (fig. 66), as well as of the legendary Bull of Heaven, and an enigmatic depiction of what the archaeologists named "The Celestial Guardian"—the image of a man against a starry sky (fig. 67).

The inscriptions, the statues, and the principal murals in the royal palace and in the remains of temples made it clear that, in the second phase of Mari's greatness, the dominant deity was the goddess whom the Sumerians called Inanna and the Akkadian/Semitic peoples called Ishtar. She was not just a deity to be worshipped; she was actively involved in Mari's affairs. Exquisite murals painted on palace walls showed her conducting the ceremony at which it was she who invested the new kings

Figure 66

Figure 67

(one of them called Zimri-Lim, "a singer to gods"; fig. 68) with the prerogatives of kingship by granting him the royal insignia. Resumed excavations in the 1950s and the 1970s confirmed that the palaces and courtyards were literally art galleries and the unearthings were expanded to both sacred and residential parts of the city.

It was certain that the statue that had captured my attention was that of Inanna/Ishtar. But in the absence of an inscription on the statue itself, it came to be known as The Goddess With A Vase. Photographs of the statue could be found in some textbooks on the history or art of the ancient Near East. The photographs invariably showed her from the front, holding a vase, which explains the naming (plate 22). The photographs show her wearing a see-through dress and a helmet ("headdress," in archaeologists' parlance) adorned with a pair of horns—the distinguishing

Figure 68

detail in ancient Near Eastern representations of divinity, a god or a goddess.

Other than the exceptional artistry at such an early time and the goddess's beauty conveyed by the statue, there seemed nothing out of the ordinary here. But when one could find a rare photograph of this statue from the back, there appeared remarkable features (fig. 69). Thus seen, the headdress was an elaborate helmet; the divine "horns" curved on the sides to become or resemble earphones. A boxlike object was attached with straps to the neck and the back of the helmet; it must have been heavy, because it was supported on the shoulders by thick protective pads. All that was held firmly in place by crossed straps that ran back and front. And a hose, hanging down from the box, ran almost the length of the statue.

In the few instances when the statue's back was shown, and in the even fewer instances when an explanation was offered, it was suggested that the hose was a kind of hocus-pocus used by the priests: They would pour in water in the back, and through the hose the water would spout in the

Figure 69

front from the vase held by the goddess, creating the illusion that the goddess was responding to prayers for long life with a spout of Waters of Life.

To my eyes, however, all these accoutrements—helmet, earphones, instrument box, extended hose—looked like the equipment of a pilot or astronaut. Numerous texts spoke of Inanna/Ishtar's love of roaming in Earth's skies. The Epic of Gilgamesh, the famed Sumerian king from Uruk, tells of how she watched from her Skychamber his efforts to reach the Landing Place of the gods. It was she who recommended for kingship the man who became known as Sargon I of Akkad after she landed her Skychamber in his field (and liked the sex that followed). A Sumerian text describes how she outwitted her great-uncle Enki and stole from him the ME—miniature tablets that held the formulas for civilization—then escaped in her "celestial boat." Hymns to her described how she "joyfully roamed the skies like a winged bird." A depiction of her in Assyria showed her as a helmeted pilot; she was often depicted as a Winged Goddess (fig. 70).

Of particular relevance to interpreting the Mari statue, I felt, was a list in a well-known Sumerian text of the seven items of attire and equipment that she wore in preparation for a long distance trip. These included the *shugarra* that she put on her head, "measuring pendants" on her ears, chains of blue stones around her neck, twin supports on her shoulders, straps that clasped her breast, and the *pala* garment that clothed her body.

Figure 70

What she held in her hands has been translated by scholars as either a "golden cylinder" or a "golden ring."

It seemed that the text matched the details in the Mari statue; but to be sure, I needed more precise and detailed photographs. The statue was kept in the Archaeological Museum in Aleppo, Syria. So I went ahead and wrote to the Museum, asking for the photographs. I stated in my letter that I would, of course, pay for the photographs and for any other costs involved.

To my great surprise—because I really did not expect to hear back from the Aleppo Museum—I received a friendly and affirmative letter, signed by its director, Nazem Djabri. That was in June 1975. I can recount these details because Mr. Djabri thoughtfully placed, on the envelope bearing his reply, stamps from a series that depicted statues from the Aleppo Museum—and I kept the envelopes. Yes, he informed me, the Museum had the statue of The Goddess With The Vase; yes, they could take photographs and send them to me at a cost of so much per photo; and was there anything else in the Museum I was interested in?

After some exchanges, I received in the ensuing months photographs not only of the goddess but of many other artifacts in the museum; I returned most of them and paid for what I kept. Enlargements of the photographs and precise sketches made me confident that the statue showed Inanna/Ishtar as a flying goddess, that the hose was part of her pilot's equipment and not for spouting water. I would have preferred to be able to actually see and examine the statue, but in the aftermath of the warfare in the Middle East that was not possible. So I included a discussion of the statue in my first book, *The 12th Planet* (1976), based on the photographs at hand.

But then I had a terrific idea: If I could not go to the statue, could the statue come to me? The publisher of my book, Sol Stein of Stein & Day, agreed that it would make a great promotion to have an author's tour in the United States with the statue at my side. I broached the idea to Mr. Djabri in Aleppo. Well, he answered, the statue cannot leave Syria, but he happened to have an exact full-sized replica of it, and he could send that to the United States if he were to accompany it. He sent photographs. The "replica" looked awful; besides, the whole value of the idea was based on authenticity: Here is how a goddess looked 4,000 years ago, as she was discovered by archaeologists—helmet, earphones, black box, hose, and all.

So the statue never came to me. I had to wait more than twenty years for the opportunity to go to the statue, but go to it I did.

✳✳✳

In 1998, after extensive preparations and based on reports that a temporary political-military calm offered a window of opportunity, I put together, with the help of Abbas Nadim and his Visions Travel & Tours organization, a once-in-a-lifetime Earth Chronicles Expedition titled SYRIA PLUS. The "Syria" of the tour program was most comprehensive; the "Plus" was a dream destination: across the border, in Lebanon, the colossal ruins of Baalbek.

We arrived in Aleppo on the seventh day of the grand tour. Syria's second largest city and its most cosmopolitan commercial hub is called Halab in Arabic; it is so mentioned in cuneiform inscriptions from the second millennium B.C. The principal deities worshiped there in antiquity were Adad (the Sumerian Ishkur, the youngest son of Enlil) and Ishtar (the Sumerian Inanna, Adad's niece). The mound where their temples had stood was used later by successive conquerors to superimpose their own temples, churches, and mosques. Now, looking over the city as The Citadel, the remaining structures date mostly to the 12th century A.D.

We arrived late in the evening and the next morning we were off to the Aleppo Museum. I inquired about Mr. Nazem Djabri, but the name meant nothing to the guards and clerks at the entrance. Only one old-timer recalled that, yes, there used to be such a director once, but now there was a new one. I asked to say hello to the current director, but he was "not in today."

We were, except for a group of schoolgirls, the only visitors in the sprawling museum, and we made a beeline for the statue. Hearts throbbed as we approached the magnificent white limestone statue. I, and all with me, looked at it, gazed at the goddess, circled the statue to examine it from all sides, climbed on chairs to peek into the top of the hose (where water was supposed to be poured in), and took all the photographs we wanted (plates 23 and 24). The guards, who at first protested, were shown the permit we obtained in Damascus to inspect and photograph at any Syrian museum or site.

The official museum guidebook, describing the statue as a "fertility goddess," explained that "in her hands she is holding a tilted vase from which, by means of piping within the statue, water could be made to flow down her fish-decorated skirt." However, we could find no openings through which water could be poured in. Undoubtedly, the notion that water could spout out of the vase held by the goddess was induced by the

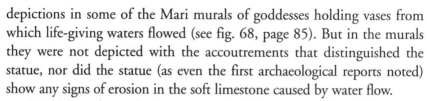

depictions in some of the Mari murals of goddesses holding vases from which life-giving waters flowed (see fig. 68, page 85). But in the murals they were not depicted with the accoutrements that distinguished the statue, nor did the statue (as even the first archaeological reports noted) show any signs of erosion in the soft limestone caused by water flow.

No matter how closely we examined the statue, the helmet, earphones, neck box, shoulder pads, the crisscrossing straps, and the hose all bespoke other functions and attributes than those of a "fertility goddess."

To me, and to those who were with me, she was and remains *The Goddess Who Roamed the Skies*—a physical being, one who actually did all that the tales of the Anunnaki described.

We spent a few more hours in the museum, admiring its collection of artifacts from bygone civilizations. The most exquisite and numerous ones were from Mari. There were statues of its governors and kings; of noblemen and women elaborately attired and coifed; ivory inlays showing soldiers, farmers, merchants; and more of the same in whatever remained of the opulent murals. I left it for a future Briefing Session to discuss some of the sculptures, the information in the clay tablets, and the significance of the cylinder seals.

The next step was to see the Mari site itself.

***

To reach Mari we drove in a great semi-circle from northwestern Syria to its southeastern-most part; the way wound mostly on the western side of the Euphrates River, but sometimes crossed to the east due to road conditions or stopover needs, then returned to the western side. Reaching the modern town of Deir-ez-Zur, we settled in the luxurious Cham Palace Hotel. In the evening's Briefing Session, I reviewed for the group what we had seen in both the Damascus and Aleppo museums that was relevant to our expedition the next day. I pointed out to them that the region where we were was where, on the eastern side of the Euphrates, it was joined by the Khabur River. It was there, I reminded my co-explorers, that the Prophet Ezekiel, having been exiled there with other Judean noblemen by the Babylonians, had the vision of the Divine Chariot.

Driving south the next morning, we were alone on the road virtually all the time. Where a dirt road began to the left, there was a rusting sign announcing MARI, with a painting of The Goddess on it. A lot of camera film was spent there to commemorate the event (plate 25). After a short ride toward where the river had once been (it has shifted eastward over the millennia), we reached the ruins.

The word *ruins* is used here most figuratively. At other archaeological sites—not just in Syria but in Turkey to the north, Jordan and Israel to the south, Lebanon to the east, and all the way to distant Egypt, Greece, and Crete—palaces and temples were built of stones. Here, at this westernmost capital of Sumer, it was mud bricks that were used as the building material—as was the case in Sumer's principal great cities—Ur, Uruk, Nippur, and so on. And, subjected to the elements, almost all that was above ground crumbled. Here, at Mari, standing remains of the sacred temples and royal palaces rose as if from the dead when the archaeologists unearthed them, as photographs from the digging reports show (fig. 71). But once those remains were exposed to the elements by the archaeologists' spades, the erosion resumed.

Figure 71

To save some of what had been discovered, the Syrian authorities built a kind of shack over the principal section of the great palace of Mari (plate 26). A path led from ground level down to the excavated area under the glass roofing. We found ourselves inside some of the 300-plus chambers, halls, and cellars of the palace, following this or that corridor as if in a labyrinth. The walls that once bore the exquisite murals, painted over their plastering, were bare. It was heartbreaking to realize that at a mere touch, the mud bricks at the touched spot would turn to dust.

As we left the below-surface covered section and emerged above ground into sunlight, there were protruding ruins wherever one looked. The ancient city occupied an area vaster than one can conceive. Here and there stone steps led to a no longer existing building. Here and there stone steps led down to a structure not yet excavated or to one that was covered again by sand and soil. Here and there a shard—a piece of pottery—lay about; those who cared picked up some, a kind of memorabilia from the Mari That Was. And except for the sound of our voices, not even a wind disturbed the utter silence of the place.

At the entrance to the site there was a sizable shack, with a table and benches. The sole guard said sure, you can sit there in the shade. We ate the box lunches the hotel had prepared for us. Some went back to take more pictures; most could not hold back their excitement at actually, really, being in Mari. It was fortunate, I thought, that we had been to the museum before coming here, or else it would be just the dusty ruins that our memories would associate with Mari.

I took the opportunity to make an important point. Who was with me in Troy? I asked, and some raised their hands. There, I said, the lesson was that the discovery of Troy and its artifacts proved the veracity of Homer's tale: There was such a city, there was a King Priam, there were the heroes and demigods, and thus, why not also accept that the gods were also there, real and not a myth? So now we are here, and we can be certain that there had been a Mari; the clay tablets in the royal archive name its kings, and we had seen some of their statues in the museum; we have seen depictions of Mari's people—and the archaeologists accept all of them as a reality. And we have also seen the statue of a goddess; but when it comes to that, the scholars say: The gods were a myth, they were just figments of imagination. . . .

Let me tell you, I went on, about what was found written in some of the tablets. During the first phase of Mari's greatness, before the demise of Sumer & Akkad, the main deity worshipped here was called Dagan—

an epithet in the local dialect that most scholars believe referred to Enlil, and which some think was another name for Adad. In the second phase, beginning more than a century after Sumer's demise, the principal deity was Ishtar; Dagan retired—yes, retired—to a nearby town called Terqa, where a temple-home was built for him.

Around 1790 B.C. Hammurabi ascended the throne in Babylon, where the national god was Marduk. The royal correspondence on the clay tablets reveals that at first he made nice with Mari, benefiting from Mari's wealth and commercial prowess; but then he began to harass Mari and its trade routes. Skirmishes turned to warfare, and he attacked and sacked the city in 1760 B.C.

The clay documents that have survived show that in the beginning the god Dagan was consulted by the kings of Mari with the aid of oracle priestesses in Dagan's temple. But toward the end, as the kings of Mari sought to pacify Babylon rather than fight as Dagan had advised, they began to neglect the god. One day, as a traveler stopped at Dagan's temple in Terqa, the god spoke up and said: Why have they stopped consulting me? Why am I no longer informed about the battles? The god's words were reported by the traveler to the governor of Terqa; he reported it to the king of Mari. The tablet with this report was found in the ruins of Mari's royal archive.

You are not making it up? someone asked. No, I said, you can find the text of the tablets representing the correspondence regarding the god Dagan in the relevant textbooks.

And after a moment of silence, I added: No writer of mythical science fiction, I think, could have invented the episode of a retired god complaining that he is no longer consulted.

Mari, more than Troy, proved the physical reality of the ancient gods.

7

UFO IN A BURIED
SYNAGOGUE

To find oneself inside a synagogue that was buried nearly 2,000 years ago is, to say the least, an eerie and unusual experience. To find therein a depiction of an angel hovering in the skies in a celestial chamber—a UFO—is certainly an astonishing surprise. And to have it all happen in Damascus, the capital of a country that is a sworn enemy of Israel, was bizarre.

Yet it all did happen when I toured Syria with a group of fans in late summer 1998.

The story begins not in Damascus but some 280 miles to the east, on the banks of the Euphrates River, at an ancient city called Dura ("The Walled City"). From an unknown early time, Dura served as a site for crossing the river and as a transfer point for people and goods from Mesopotamia and beyond in the East to the Mediterranean and beyond in the West. Its recorded history dates to about 300 B.C. in the reign of Seleucus I Nicanor, Alexander's general who assumed control of the Asiatic parts of Alexander's empire after the Macedonian's death. The city was henceforth known as Dura-Europos, perhaps in honor of the birthplace of Seleucus, Europus in Macedonia.

A century later, when Rome was the imperial power, Dura-Europos became the easternmost garrisoned outpost of Roman rule. A thriving commercial center, it was a desired prize by marauding hosts, but it was

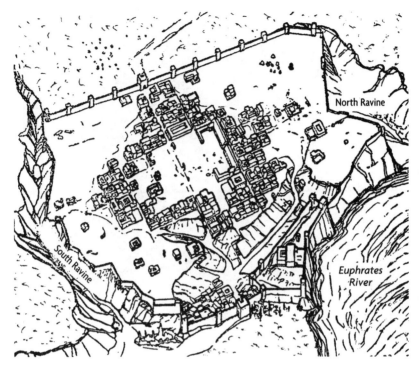

Figure 72

not easy to capture: On the east it was protected by the wide Euphrates River; on the north and south, it was protected by deep and wide natural ravines; and on the west it was protected by a massive defensive wall (fig. 72).

As Parthians and then Sassanians from Persia/Iran kept challenging the Roman legions, the defenders of Dura-Europos refortified the city in an unusual way: They filled all the buildings that abutted the city's wall, on the west, with desert sand—creating a massive rampart that was intended to make the western fortifications unbreachable. Yet, in 256 A.D., the Sassanian hordes managed to capture the city and razed it to the ground. Its ruins lay abandoned and forgotten until a company of British soldiers happened upon the place in the aftermath of World War I. Digging for emplacements to garrison themselves among some protruding ruins, they uncovered (as the report from that time stated) "some ancient wall paintings in a wonderful state of preservation."

The report reached the archaeologist James Henry Breasted, who was surveying ancient sites in Iraq and choosing sites meriting excavation. In

Figure 73

time, the French Academy and Yale University joined forces to conduct excavations throughout the 1920s and 1930s. And what they discovered was nothing less than a Near Eastern "Pompeii"—intact ancient dwellings and public edifices buried, not by volcanic ash as in Pompeii, but by dry desert sand.

The extensive excavations revealed that Dura-Europos was a cosmopolitan city, where local residents and garrisoned soldiers mingled with traders and travelers from many lands and of varied faiths. Judging by depictions and dedicatory inscriptions in Greek, Aramaic, Latin, Palmyrene, Iranian, and other tongues, the city had temples or places of worship for a full range of deities—temples to Zeus and Artemis; Bel and the Moon god; the Triad of Palmyra; the Parthian god Aphlad and the Iranian god Mithra (in whose shrine the legend of his slaying of the heavenly bull was depicted by a wall sculpture; fig. 73). A Jewish synagogue and a Christian place of worship were there too.

Best preserved of all was the section of the city where its defenders, some 1,800 years earlier, had buried the buildings abutting the city's defensive wall on the west with sand. When the sand was removed, the roofless buildings saw again the light of day and the wall paintings that decorated them could again be seen as they had been.

The city's synagogue, which was expanded from an earlier structure to a larger and more elevated house of prayer (fig. 74), was located just one short city block from the town's main gate, and was thus one of the buildings along the defensive wall that were completely covered with sand to reinforce the fortifications by extending and raising the ramparts (fig. 75). As a result, when the archaeologists removed the sand, the wall of the synagogue where the Scrolls of the Law (the Torah) were kept remained almost fully intact, while the two side walls had their tops sliced off diagonally.

The walls, the excavators discovered, were used as canvases for murals in vivid colors that illustrated major events and personalities from the Old Testament—the tales of the Patriarchs, of the Exodus; scenes from

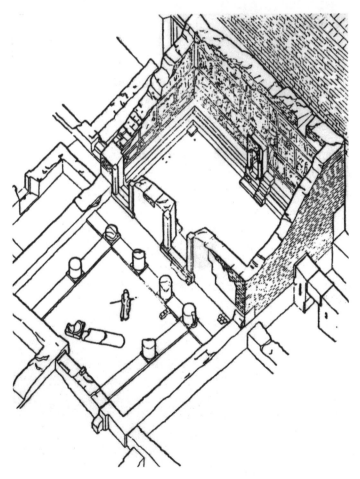

Figure 74

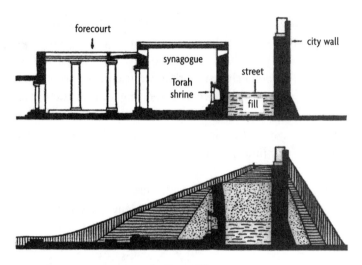

Figure 75

the books of Judges and Kings; and on through the Book of Esther in later times. Influenced by the Greco-Roman art styles, the artists ignored the prohibition against depicting anthropomorphic images and showed the personalities dressed as befits the artists' time.

In order to preserve these remarkable wall paintings and make them more accessible to scholars, they were carefully removed and transferred to the National Museum in Damascus. One could, however, spend days in that great museum without ever encountering the Dura-Europos wall paintings; for, as I and my group found out when we went to the museum, the paintings were not on display in any of the museum's galleries. Only after some insistence that we wanted see them was our group led to an open courtyard in a remote part of the museum, at the edge of which there was a nondescript old house with two low doorways. "It's there," the guide said.

When we entered the house, we were dumbstruck. We found ourselves viewing the ancient paintings inside a reconstruction of the synagogue itself: The walls with their paintings were re-erected to resurrect the synagogue itself, as were the floor and the stone benches at the base of the walls. It was an eerie experience; for a while we all just stood there, frozen and speechless as though we were part of the excavated mute walls.

It took some time—probably not more than a few minutes but minutes that felt like a long time—for us to shake ourselves into the reality of the present. We then started to move about, coming closer to the walls, taking a closer look at the painted panels, or moving back away from this or that wall to gain a more panoramic view of the ancient artwork. Awkward hesitation gave way to recognition: Here was Moses at the Burning Bush, with the Divine Presence intimated by showing only the Hand of God (fig. 76). Here was his brother Aaron, identified by his name, written in Greek. Scenes of the Exodus showed Israelites and Egyptians, each group distinguished by their different garments. King David was depicted in several panels; the biblical tale of the Philistines bringing the captured Ark of the Covenant to their temple, only to see the statues of their gods fall before it, was shown (fig. 77). Other panels depicted the miracles performed by the Prophet Elijah. As in a comic strip, episodes connected with the Prophet Ezekiel were depicted on adjoining panels; there, as elsewhere, the divine intervention was depicted by showing only the Hand of God, floating above the scene.

The almost fully intact west wall contained a score of panels with the most important biblical episodes. An arched niche in its center, placed at the top of a raised platform reachable by a few steps, was obviously a built-in ark to hold the Torah (plate 27). The paintings surrounding it

Figure 76

Figure 77

were designed so as to create the illusion that it was three dimensional, flanked by two virtual columns. Above the columns and the arched niche the paintings showed the presumed facade of the Temple in Jerusalem. One could see next to it the Menorah, the Temple's candelabra, and other symbols of Jewish ritual.

The scene to the left of the painted Temple facade (to the right of the viewer facing the wall) depicted the tale of the Testing of Abraham. He was told by God to take his son Isaac to Mount Moriah and there offer him as a burnt sacrifice as proof of Abraham's unquestioning faith in the only God; but as Abraham was about to apply the knife to his son, an Angel of the Lord suddenly appeared and called to him from the skies to stop. What had happened can best be told in the Bible's own words:

> And when Abraham put forth his hand
> and took the knife to slaughter his son,
> It was then that an angel of the Lord
> called to him from the sky, saying:
> Abraham! Abraham!
> And he answered: Here I am!
> And the angel said:
> Lay not your hand upon the lad,
> for now I know that thou fearest God,

since thou did not withhold from Me thy son!
And Abraham looked and saw a ram caught
in the thicket by its horns,
And Abraham sacrificed the ram
instead of his son.

As the group spread out to whatever panel caught their interest or looked best for picture taking, I drifted toward the partly damaged north wall. One of its panels, which had only partially survived because of the diagonal slant of the sand-filled ramp, showed Jacob's nighttime dream-vision of angels ascending and descending a ladder that connected the ground to the skies. The simplistic depiction from 2,000 years ago reminded me how I, and other children in our Bible class, used to draw the scene. I smiled, bemused: Here, in the capital of Syria, a persistent enemy of the State of Israel, was preserved a depiction of Jacob, grandson of Abraham, whose name was changed to Israe-El after he wrestled an angel, originating the name Israel.

I sometimes used the tale of Jacob's Dream in lectures, as a way to answer the question, Do you believe in UFOs? In answer I would tell the audience: Imagine that the door to this hall opens and a young man bursts in, shouting, Hold everything! I must tell you what has happened to me! Excited and out of breath, he tells us that he was hiking from his hometown to another distant town to find a bride. Darkness fell; he was tired and lay down to sleep in the field. In the middle of the night he was awakened by noises and bright lights. Half asleep, half blinded by the lights, he saw a UFO! It hovered above ground; he could see a ladder coming down from it; some of its occupants were going up and down it. Silhouetted against a light inside, he could see someone standing at the doorway or open hatch, perhaps the craft's commander.

Overcome with awe, frightened, the young man fainted. When he came to, the UFO was gone, the commander was gone, the ladder was gone, and all who were upon it were gone—as though it was all a dream. But, the young man who burst into the hall insists: It was not a dream. I actually saw it all after I was awakened; I even heard the commander speaking to me, it was real!

Now—I would ask the audience—should we believe this young man's tale? Was he pulling our leg, or was it all just a dream, or did he actually have an encounter with a UFO and its occupants?

My own answer is: This was one UFO story about which I had no doubts, because it is the biblical tale of Jacob's Dream; except that to Jacob it was not an encounter with an *Unidentified* Flying Object—to him it was a Divine Encounter, and he well knew whom he had encountered. They were *Malachim,* translated as "angels," but literally meaning "emissaries," of the *Elohim,* translated as "God," but a plural word for "divine beings."

Figure 78

As I stood inside the excavated synagogue of Dura-Europos, reminiscing about, I wondered how the artist depicted the divine vehicle in the mural's obliterated part. It was then that someone shouted: Hey, you must come to see this!

He was pointing to the section, on the west wall, dealing with the Testing of Abraham. The comprehensive scene (fig. 78) showed the unfolding events: The stone altar, the wood for the fire, Isaac upon the altar, Abraham ready with the sacrificial knife, the ram caught in the thicket, and the Hand of God representing divine intervention.

But there was an additional element in the depiction, the one that caused the shout: The other participant in the event, the Angel of the Lord, was shown as a humanlike figure standing at the opening of an oval-shaped structure (fig. 79). It is not a tent; it is not a house (for we know how abodes of the time looked). It is shown at the painting's top,

Figure 79

Figure 80

the skies from where the angel called out to Abraham; it is shown next to the Hand-of-God.

And we all, at once, had the same thought as the shouter who first noticed it: Was the millennia-old painting depicting that time's notion of a Divine Chariot—what is nowadays described as an Unidentified Flying Object, a UFO?

This is definitely not how, in Jewish traditional folk art, the angel in this biblical event is depicted, I said. The angel is depicted therein as anthropomorphic, with wings (example, fig. 80). But here, in a depiction closer by 2,000 years to the events, the angel is within a "flying chamber"!

That evening, back at the hotel, I suggested to the group that we look up some of the illustrations in my book *The Stairway to Heaven* depicting the Flying Chambers of the ancient gods. The one most pertinent was that of the Ben-Ben, the Celestial Boat in which Egypt's great god Ra had arrived on Earth. The scale model, made of stone (fig. 81a), clearly showed the craft's commander standing at its open doorway or hatch, very much like the depiction in Dura-Europos. In my book it was presented alongside the image of an early type Command Module used by NASA (fig. 81b).

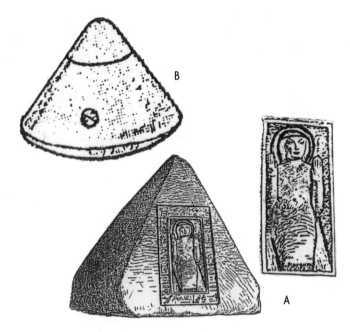

Figure 81

These, and other illustrations in my books, showed obvious similarities to the depiction at Dura-Europos; and we were all convinced that we had indeed seen a UFO depicted on the west wall of the buried synagogue.

***

The tale of Dura-Europos and its wall paintings would not be complete without relating our subsequent visit to the site of Dura-Europos and its environs.

As one who had made a point of visiting and seeing with my own eyes, both physically and emotionally, the ancient sites and exhibited artifacts I was writing about whenever such a visit was feasible, I insisted that the Syria itinerary include the hardly ever visited sites of Mari and Dura-Europos, as out of the way as they were (see map, fig. 82).

To achieve that we made a great semi-circle, driving from Aleppo eastward to reach the Euphrates River, and then in a southeasterly direction along the River, crossing and recrossing it several times until we reached Deir-ez-Zur—a commercial hub deemed to be the center of Syria's "oil industry." We settled in the Furat Cham Palace Hotel, a truly

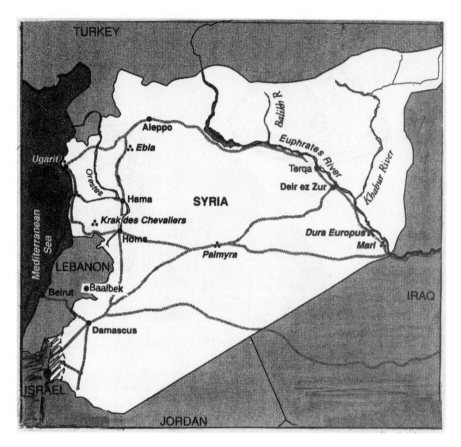

Figure 82

palatial hotel with marble everywhere; located on the town's outskirts, it was touted as the hotel where all the executives of major oil companies stay. (I recall wondering at the time why executives of international oil companies would come there when Syria's few oil wells, east of the Euphrates, hardly make it a player in the international oil trade. The answer came to light during the Iraq War in 2003: A pipeline downstream secretly delivered contraband Iraqi oil to Syria, which then exported the crude oil as its own.)

Although Dura-Europos is closer to Deir-ez-Zur, we drove first to Mari; and only after the memorable visit there drove back north to the ruins of Dura-Europos. With the protective sands (and the murals) removed, all we could see were the crumbling remains of the city's fortifications, the remains of some walls, and columns; there were stone pavements all over the place (plate 28). A guard on a motorcycle appeared from nowhere carrying a rifle, shooting it now and then as though target practicing (but in reality, we assumed, to impress on us the need to pay him a sizable gratuity—which we did).

With his help, we located where the synagogue had been. There was not much left to be seen. Even the best imagination, and sketches I had with me, failed to inspire. But it made at least visually clear what the biblical Lamentations meant when they bewailed a city that was once full of people now sitting desolate, abandoned. Yet it is at such places as Mari and Dura-Europos, rather than when seeing antiquities in the midst of a bustling city, that one truly witnesses history's turning Wheel of Fortune.

I got up very early the next morning; all were still asleep. I went out to the hotel's large terrace overlooking the river. I pulled up a chair and sat at a vantage point from where I could see where the river made a bend; the view was breathtaking (plate 29).

I was thinking of the depictions in the Dura-Europos synagogue, of the image of the UFO, of Abraham. When Abraham's family left Ur in southern Mesopotamia for Harran, now in southeastern Turkey near the border with Syria, they had to cross the Euphrates River *somewhere*. . . . In the twenty-first century B.C., Mari was the place of crossing; then it was at Dura-Europos; now it is at Deir-ez-Zur. Was it here, perhaps, at this forlorn stretch of the river, that my ancestor had passed on a journey that led to the One God?

And there, alone on the terrace overlooking the Euphrates, I was seized with a sense of history and ancestry that I shall never forget.

8

ELIJAH'S WHIRLWINDS

In my first book, *The 12th Planet* (1976), I devoted a whole chapter to the flying vehicles—spacecraft, shuttlecraft, aircraft—of the Anunnaki (the biblical *Nefilim*) and their names, descriptions, and depictions in antiquity. The Sumerians spoke of Divine Birds and depicted rocketships; the Egyptians had hymns to the gods' Celestial Boat or Heavenly Barque and found ways to depict them. The Hebrew Bible (Old Testament) spoke of "whirlwinds." The Prophet Ezekiel, walking along the Khabur River (see map, page 106), saw (as told in the first chapter of his Book):

> A Whirlwinds coming from the north
> as a great cloud with flashes of fire
> and brilliance all around it;
> And within it, from within the fire,
> there was a radiance like a glowing halo.

The Whirlwind was described as resting upon four extensions which, equipped with wheels, enabled it to move in all directions, and it had a rim of "eyes." This description led me to compare Ezekiel's Whirlwind to bulbous objects, with extended legs and "eyes," that were found depicted on wall paintings at an archaeological site called Tell-Ghassul in Jordan (fig. 83).

The Prophet Elijah, some three centuries before Ezekiel, not only

Figure 83

saw such a divine chariot, but was actually taken aloft in it. As related in II Kings 2:

> There appeared a chariot of fire
> with fiery horses . . .
> And Elijah went up to heaven
> in a Whirlwind.

In the case of Elijah, there is no detail regarding the shape of the Whirlwind, except that we are given to understand that it appeared from the skies, descended low enough to pick up Elijah, and then swooped back upward and disappeared from view. Elijah's disciple and successor Elisha witnessed it all.

However, we are given for that happening a detailed indicator of the geography of the place. The Prophet, his chief disciple, and other disciples were journeying from Judea eastward, toward the Jordan River—all aware that Elijah had an appointment to be taken aloft. Reaching Jericho, Elijah asked all others to stay behind, but none did. When he reached the Jordan River, he made clear that he must cross it alone, but while the others stood back, Elisha persisted and followed his master. Once they were across and the two walked on, the fiery chariot, the Whirlwind, appeared and carried Elijah off.

The encounter with the Whirlwind thus took place on the eastern side of the Jordan River, opposite Jericho, and not far from the river itself—Elisha recrossed the river at the same crossing point right after the occurrence.

The similarity between the divine vehicles depicted at Tell-Ghassul and the biblical Whirlwinds prompted me to do some extensive research on that archaeological site; the results were detailed by me in my 1985 book *The Wars of Gods and Men*. The excavations at the site, I found out, were begun in 1929 by an archaeological mission organized by the Vatican's Pontifical Biblical Institute. The archaeologists, led by Alexis Mallon, discovered that the mound consisted of habitations on three hillocks, of which two were used for residences and one as a work area.

The archaeological team was surprised by the high level of civilization found there: Even the oldest habitations, at a period that stretched from the end of the Stone Age to the Bronze Age, were paved with bricks. Houses were rectangular in layout and grouped as in a modern suburb (fig. 84), and, most amazingly, the walls inside were covered with multi-colored murals.

In one instance the house contained a recessed divan so built that it enabled the occupant to see the painting on the opposite wall while reclining. The mural depicted two seated figures facing a row of attendants or worshippers, and a person stepping out of an object emitting rays. In another mural, a rayed eight-pointed star-like design in vivid colors was

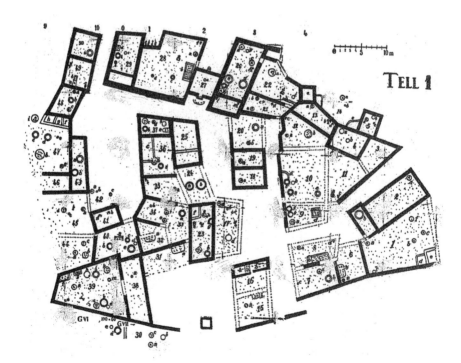

Figure 84

Figure 85

executed with great geometric precision (fig. 85). And in another there appeared the black bulbous "whirlwinds" with the extended supports or legs, and "eyes."

Tell-Ghassul, I found, was located a short distance from the Jordan River on its eastern bank (see map, fig. 86), directly opposite Jericho on the western side of the river. In the words of the archaeologists who continued excavating until 1933:

> From atop the mound, one has an interesting all-around-view: the Jordan on the west as a dark line; to the northwest, the hillock of ancient Jericho; and beyond it, the mountains of Judea.

It all sounded very much like the place where Elijah had gone to be taken aloft. That meant that at first opportunity I had to go there and see it all with my own eyes.

That first opportunity came about in the winter of 1995, when I included Jordan in an Earth Chronicles Expedition. Arriving via Cairo, we stayed in Amman, Jordan's capital, from where we made visits to various

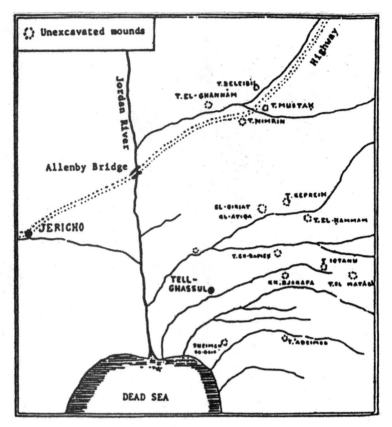

Figure 86

sites in Jordan. The very first morning we went to the National Archaeological Museum to see the Tell-Ghassul murals, for I presumed that they were kept there. But there were no such murals in the Museum, and no one even knew what I was talking about.

In the evening we were invited to a reception at ACOR (American Center of Oriental Research) in Amman, and I made inquiries there. No one knew anything about the murals, but someone knew about a place called Tell-Ghassul. There are archaeologists from the University of Sydney, Australia, working there now, I was told.

We were provided with directions for how to get to the site, and our tour bus drove us there the next morning. Other than the fact that it rose somewhat above the landscape, it was only the sight of some people moving about that suggested that this was the place. I introduced myself and my group to the man in charge, indeed an archaeologist from Australia.

What made you come to this place? I asked. He wasn't sure, saying it was a decision made by others. What are you looking for? I asked. He explained that someone felt that the excavators sixty years ago had merely scratched the ground and there was much more to be found with modern methods. The few people on his team were digging deeper trenches, looking for remains of stone structures. You can roam around as you wish, he told us; any shards (pottery fragments) that you see are thousands of years old; you can take what you want.

My fans spread out, picked up pottery shards, took them back to Amman (and the United States). I went about seeking the highest spot on the mound, from which I gazed out westward. The view was indeed as the archaeologists described it sixty years before: In the shimmering sunlight, one could see what could only be Jericho. Tell-Ghassul could well be the place where Elijah was taken aloft by the Whirlwind (plate 30).

Before leaving, I went to say good-bye and thank the archaeologist from Sydney. By the way, I said, do you know what happened to the murals found here in the 1930s? Oh, I think they were transferred to the Rockefeller Museum in Jerusalem, he said.

***

The Rockefeller Archaeological Museum is located just outside the walls of Jerusalem's Old City, near Herod's Gate. During the British Mandate over Palestine, I visited the Museum two or three times to see what was then one of the best collections of Holy Land antiquities. When that part of Jerusalem was under Jordanian rule (1948–1967), it also housed most of the Dead Sea scrolls, which had by then been discovered. After the Six Day War in 1967, the Museum also served as the headquarters of the Israel Antiquities Authority.

It did not take me long after the return from Jordan to contact the Rockefeller Museum in Jerusalem, now part of Israel, and inquire about the Tell-Ghassul murals. The eventual reply said, in essence, What murals? In the absence of the Chief Curator, no one had any idea what I was inquiring about. Try the Albright Institute, they said.

I contacted the W. F. Albright Institute of Archaeological Research in Jerusalem, so named after the late great archaeologist of the Lands of the Bible. Trying to be helpful, they checked with this or that institute and finally came back with an answer: Try the Pontifical Biblical Institute in Jerusalem—after all, it was they who were given the task by the Vatican to organize the excavations. Feeling that I was getting hot on the mural's trail, I asked the Expeditions tour operator, Visions Travel & Tours of Los Angeles, to set in motion a group tour to Israel.

When contact was finally established with a Person-in-Charge at the Pontifical Institute, I was told that the Institute did house some of the Tell-Ghassul paintings, but they were in such a state of disintegration that they had been put in boxes and sent to the Israel Museum in Jerusalem for restoration. I was given the name of the Chief Restorer, Mrs. Osnat Brandl, and lost no time contacting her. She wrote back, after returning from her annual vacation, that there had been discussions about transferring the artifacts, but they had not been not sent over yet.

With an Earth Chronicles Expedition to Israel taking shape, I dropped the exchanges by letter and fax and started to call Jerusalem urgently. Back at the Pontifical Institute, I was told that the Institute had closed down for the summer, and that the person who really would know anything, Father Fulco, had gone to spend a year with a Jesuit college in California. I managed to locate him at The Jesuit Community of the Loyola Marymount University in Los Angeles. In a long fax dated Friday 29 August 1997, he informed me that "the TG frescoes are in the mezzanine storeroom in wooden cases with glass covers" at the Pontifical Institute; "smaller fragments are in the cabinet." He had contacted Jerusalem and could assure me that Father Crocker at the Institute would facilitate the viewing of the fresco pieces and give us a pleasant welcome.

I arrived in Jerusalem with my wife ahead of the group and called the Institute to arrange the visit. My desperate fax that day to Father Fulco tells what then happened: "I called the Institute for a Monday, September 15 visit only to find out Father Crocker is also away. Father Juan Moreno who acts as caretaker knows nothing about the frescoes or how to open the Storeroom."

All the way from California Father William Fulco faxed me the name and phone number of Sandra Scham, a volunteer researcher who had assisted him. And so, when the whole group arrived at the Institute on September 15, 1997 (plate 31), she too arrived, and opened the storeroom for us!

It was cluttered with boxes, piled up on a table and on the floor, with hardly room to walk. Display cabinets along the walls held various small clay artifacts. The long table, it turned out, had a glass top on which cardboard and corrugated carton boxes were placed—evidently cartons that had been emptied of their supplies, for some were marked "Lipton's Tea" or biscuits or canned fruits; they were, I realized, the original boxes used by the excavators to ship the finds to Jerusalem. The dust suggested that no one had bothered to disturb it all for decades.

As we lifted some of the boxes off the glass-topped table, one could see that painted fragments were laid out in compartments under the glass . . . In a moment one could see the black "eye idols," as Sandra Scham called them: painted bulbous black objects with extended legs and "eyes" (plate 32).

The search was over! The "whirlwinds" that someone painted on a wall across the Jordan River thousands of years ago—the actual parts of the walls of Tell-Ghassul—were here on the display table in front of me. I lifted the glass cover and touched a fragment, only to stop at once for it was too fragile. In turns we took photographs of the fragments, of the display cabinets, of the reproductions of the rayed "star" that were painted on the room's wall above a cabinet. We saw, and photographed, history (plate 33).

The next day, by appointment authorized by the Chief Curator of the Rockefeller Museum, I went there and was taken down to an underground vault room to see the "star" (which the Museum, confronted with a copy of Father Fulco's fax, admitted it had). On a special table a large square wooden box was resting. No pictures! the Museum assistant warned me as two employees removed the box's top.

But when the top was removed, all I could see were the crumbled remains of plaster: The amazingly beautiful mural had completely disintegrated. There was nothing to photograph, even if I had been allowed.

Back at the hotel that afternoon, looking out from my room's window to the Old City, I thought of the long search for the murals and the energy and efforts it took and the ups and downs along the way and wondered whether it was all worthwhile. And I concluded that it was. I, and those who have read my books, had been able to verify that what I wrote and depicted was so.

Who was the artist who, thousands of years ago, painted the murals of Tell-Ghassul? We still don't know. Who reclined on the divan to enjoy the murals? We don't know, though in *The Wars of Gods and Men* I offered an answer. Were the depicted black bulbous objects the Whirlwinds that carried Elijah up and away? If not—what do they depict?

Was Tell-Ghassul the place where Elijah was taken heavenwards? I truly think so.

9

HOW JOSEPH SAVED EGYPT

This is a complex tale, involving seemingly unrelated ingredients: a biblical tale, a 3,800-year-old problem, enigmatic dreams by a Pharaoh, power politics in the 1960s, and an American engineer who lived in a previous century; and linking them all was my ancestor Joseph. It all led to the inclusion in an expedition to Egypt of a place where no visitor usually goes, to find the evidence of a tremendous feat of engineering and to confirm a new twist in the biblical story of how Joseph saved Egypt.

The story of Joseph in Egypt, which begins in chapter 37 of Genesis, is full of fascinating, dramatic, and mysterious aspects. Sold into bondage by his jealous half brothers because of his annoying dreams, he ends up as a male servant in the household of an official in the king's (Pharaoh's) court in Egypt. "Handsome and good looking," he caught the fancy of the official's wife; when he refused her advances, she accused Joseph of trying to seduce her and for that he was put in jail.

In the prison house he gained a reputation as a solver of dreams. And so, when the Pharaoh had a series of dreams that none of his soothsayers could explain, Joseph was brought before the king to solve them. Told that the dreams entailed seven meager cows devouring seven fat cows, seven scorched ears of grain swallowing seven healthy ears of grain, Joseph told the king his dream predicted that seven years of plentiful crops would be followed by seven years of famine. Impressed, the Pharaoh appointed Joseph Overseer in charge of the whole Land of

Egypt. Joseph—so the story goes—put in force a plan to store grain during the seven years of plenty and set it aside for the lean years. And so it was that when crops failed for seven years everywhere, "there was provision in Egypt."

Having grown up in the Middle East, I was bothered by the reported solution to the anticipated famine. There was no way, I could see with my own eyes during the shortages and rationings of World War II, to store food in the hot climate for any length of time—to say nothing of fourteen years (from the start of the storing to the end of the famine). Instead of edible grains, there would be rotting grains eaten by and filled with bugs and vermin.

With no rainfall to speak of, Egypt, true to an oft-repeated statement, is the Child of the Nile. This a visitor discovers as soon as Cairo or Luxor, which hug the Nile River, are left behind en route to visit an archaeological site: After a mile or so, one is in the desert. As one flies from Cairo to Luxor, for example, it becomes obvious from the air that the country depends on a thin ribbon of water—the Nile River—for its livelihood and existence. Irrigation canals and ditches expand the river's life-giving waters along the riverbanks; elsewhere, the landscape is yellow-brown desert.

The Nile River, one of the world's longest, begins in Ethiopia and southern Sudan and flows into the Mediterranean Sea. Its waters increase after the rainy season where it originates, creating an annual peak and then a low. But in the 1960s, when Egypt's ruler Gamal Nasser involved the superpowers in plans to build a high dam where the river enters Egypt, another aspect of the Nile's highs and lows became headline news: It turned out that the rainfall pattern at the Nile's sources was such that the Nile's waters rise and fall not only annually, but also increase and diminish in a cycle that averages *seven years*. The planned high dam (which was built and completed in 1971) was to create a huge reservoir—a virtual lake—that could retain the high-time waters and release them gradually during the low period.

That bit of information, about a seven-year cycle, loomed important to me. It seemed to corroborate the basic element in the biblical tale of Joseph's rise to power, from slave to Overseer of Egypt—the seven years of plenty (rising Nile waters) followed by seven years of shortages (falling waters). Suddenly it dawned on me that if Egypt's problem in Joseph's time was one of water, the solution had to be one of water. The repeated discussion in the media of why the dam was needed—the seven-year cycle—also offered to me the first lead to what had bothered me about the difficulties, even improbability, of storing food for fourteen years. The problem that faced Joseph, I realized, was not one of storing grain but one of *storing water!*

I owe what ensued to an American engineer and inventor named Francis Cope Whitehouse, a native of Rochester, N.Y. Looking through old reports and newspaper clippings in the New York Public Library concerning Egypt's water problem, I learned that a century earlier, in the 1860s, the British, who then ruled Egypt, had been studying ways and means of regulating the country's water supply. Among the experts invited to study the problem and offer solutions was Francis Cope Whitehouse. To do a good job, he traveled extensively along the Nile, and became intrigued by remains of ancient irrigation canals. His curiosity eventually led him to a large, thriving agricultural area some sixty miles southwest of Memphis, Egypt's ancient capital. There, in the middle of the desert, was the area called in Arabic El-Fayum. It was like an oasis in the desert, except that it was a very large oasis, and instead of a spring or well to provide water, it had a sizable *lake,* Lake Qarun. This whole area of amazing fertility lay in a natural depression, almost below sea level (see map, fig. 87).

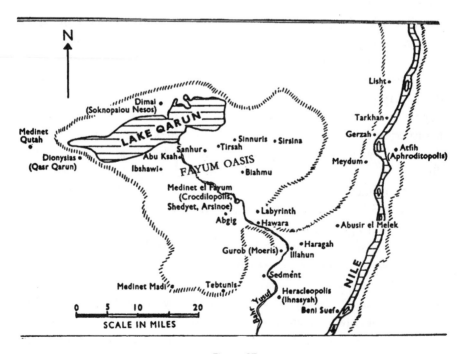

Figure 87

And what puzzled Whitehouse was this: How did this lake get its waters, in a totally arid zone and so far away (some twenty-five to thirty miles) from the Nile?

Examining the lake and its shores, Whitehouse found remains of ancient dams, quays, and other monumental structures. Back in Cairo, he searched the geographical records, recent and old. Soon he found that maps of Egypt from medieval times, based on maps prepared in antiquity by Ptolemy of Alexandria, showed that in that period the el-Fayum depression contained not one but two lakes: a more extensive Lake Keroun and an even larger lake called Moeris.

In April 1883 Whitehouse appeared before the Khedivial Geographical Society in Cairo and dropped a bombshell: He had found the answer to the el-Fayum puzzle in the writings of Herodotus (the fifth-century B.C. Greek historian-geographer). There was, Herodotus wrote, a huge lake *artificially formed* in the time of the Pharaoh Moeris. It was a lake so large that its "circumference of 3,600 furlongs equaled the entire length of Egypt along the sea coast."

Whitehouse further quoted from the writings of other ancient historians—Diodorus, Strabo, Mutianus, Pliny—to show that not only in Greek times, but also in later Roman times it was known that the whole el-Fayum depression was in fact a huge artificial lake. It was the best source of fish in Egypt, and the string of villages along its shores served as Egypt's breadbasket. But this deepened the mystery even more. If the natural el-Fayum depression was used to create an artificial lake, who was its master engineer and planner, and how was the lake kept filled with water?

Whitehouse found the first clue in the writings of Herodotus: "The water of the lake does not come out of the ground, which is here extremely dry, but is introduced by a canal from the Nile." In June 1883 Whitehouse went before the Society of Biblical Archaeology in London to announce his further discoveries. The canal that had fed the ancient Lake Moeris still partly exists, he declared. It is an artificial waterway which connects the Fayum depression with the Nile and which the Arabs still call *Bahr Yousof*—"The Waterway of Joseph"!

The announcement at the Society gathering was followed by a series of lectures and pamphlets in which Whitehouse showed a relentless dedication to the promotion of his discovery: that it was Joseph, the Hebrew Patriarch, who had conceived, planned, and carried out the colossal irrigation enterprise.

Delving into all available sources, Whitehouse found (and made his findings public) that Arab historians not only attributed the project to Joseph, but also explained the origin of the place's name. The Pharaoh's other viziers, envious of Joseph's powers, persuaded the Pharaoh to double the challenge to Joseph's engineering scheme by allowing him only a thousand days to carry it out. Beating the odds, Joseph achieved what his detractors thought impossible. He dug feeder canals and created the artificial lake in a thousand days, *Alf Yum* in Arabic. And so the place became known as the place of the thousand days, Alf Yum—*Al (or el-) Fayum*.

Whitehouse died a controversial personality in 1911; and thus was forgotten the discovery by an American engineer from Rochester that not only credited the Hebrew Patriarch with great engineering skills, but also brought to light evidence of Joseph's existence: the artificial waterworks bearing his name and the legends surrounding his feat.

∗∗∗

In the century that elapsed since the inspired revelations by Whitehouse, archaeological discoveries enabled the identification of monuments, rulers, dynasties, sites, and chronologies. Using such data to synchronize the Age of the Hebrew Patriarchs with Mesopotamian chronology, I arrived at the date of 1870 B.C. as the year of Joseph's birth (detailed in my book *The Wars of Gods and Men*). Since according to Genesis 41:46 Joseph was thirty years old when he was put in charge of preparing Egypt for the seven lean years, the year the project was launched had to be 1840 B.C.

Thus, as far as I was concerned, the way to test Whitehouse's findings was to answer this question: Who was the reigning Pharaoh at that time, and did he have any verifiable connection to the el-Fayum and its lake?

I was pleasantly surprised—no, astounded—to find that the Pharaoh at the time, Amenemhet III of the Middle Kingdom's XII dynasty, ascended the throne in 1842 B.C. (two years prior to Joseph's appointment) and reigned until his death in 1797 B.C. His records attribute to him—in the clearest manner—the development of waterworks and irrigation canals in the Fayum area. The construction there of an artificial lake was linked to him through two larger-than-life statues of him in the center of the lake. It was in his time that the Fayum area became the breadbasket of Egypt, especially known for its fresh vegetables and fruits and fish.

Plate 2. The ruins of Troy, Turkey: ancient occupation levels

Plate 1. The author and his wife at Troy by the "Trojan Horse"

Plate 3. "The headless spaceman" artifact in the Istanbul Archaeological Museum

Plate 4. The disputed artifact in the author's hand

Plate 5. "The little guy" carving on stone column, Tula, Mexico

Plate 6. The spaceman object on display in the Istanbul Archaeological Museum

Plate 7. Amid the excavated ruins of ancient Akrotiri, the island of Thera

Plate 8. Uncovered mural, Thera: A lost maritime civilization

Plate 9 (above). The Phaestos Disc, with its undeciphered writing

Plate 10 (left). The Expedition in Crete: exploring ancient Phaestos

Plate 11. Discovering traces of copper processing at Phaestos

Plate 12. The Aztec stone calendar, National Museum of Anthropology,
Mexico City

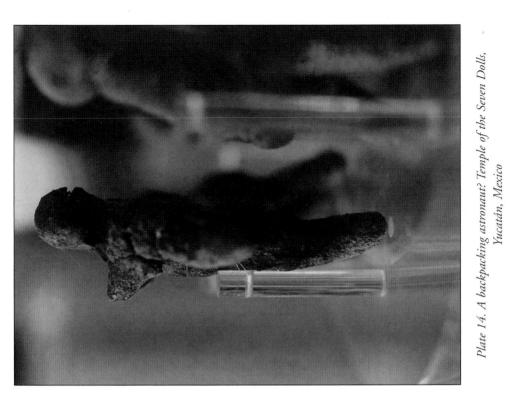

*Plate 14. A backpacking astronaut? Temple of the Seven Dolls,
Yucatán, Mexico*

*Plate 13. The sculpted stone "starman,"
Merida Museum, Yucatán, Mexico*

Plate 16. A backpacking giant: rock depiction, National Museum of Anthropology, Mexico City

Plate 15. A backpacking "angel," sculpture at Chichén Itzá, Yucatán, Mexico

Plate 17. A giant Olmec stone head, the Park Museum, Villahermosa, Yucatán, Mexico

Plate 18. The Expedition with a giant Olmec stone head in Jalapa, Mexico

Plate 19. Olmec clay toys, equipped with wheels, Anthropological Museum of the University of Veracruz, Jalapa, Mexico

Plate 20. An Olmec toy: a little elephant, Anthropological Museum of the University of Veracruz, Jalapa, Mexico. Now you see it . . .

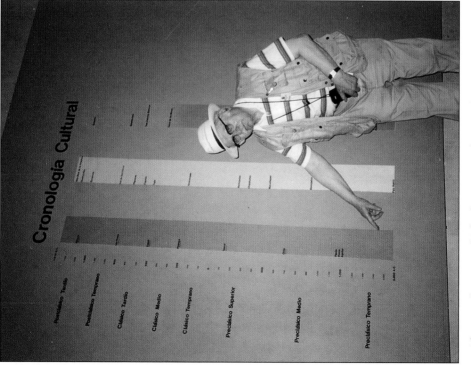

*Plate 22. The "Goddess with a Vase" discovered in Mari,
Sumer's tenth capital city*

*Plate 21. "3000 B.C." The depiction confirming the author's dating,
which later disappeared*

Plate 24. The Expedition examining the aeronautical equipment of the Flying Goddess, Archaeological Museum, Aleppo, Syria

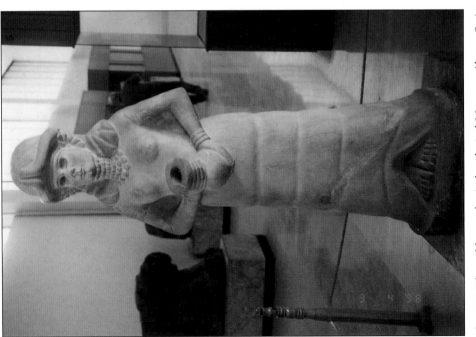

Plate 23. The goddess in the Archaeological Museum, Aleppo, Syria

Plate 25. Arriving at Mari, Syria, where the goddess crowned kings

Plate 26. Inside the royal palace's excavated remains, Mari, Syria

Plate 27 (left). The buried synagogue of Dura-Europos: the Torah niche and its murals

Plate 28 (below). Among the ruins of Dura-Europos: the site of the synagogue

Plate 29. By the banks of the Euphrates River: the view at Deir-ez-Zur, Syria

Plate 30. Where the Whirlwind snatched Elijah? At Tell-Ghassul, Jordan

Plate 31. The Pontifical Biblical Institute, Jerusalem

Plate 32. The bulbous black "Whirlwinds": finds from the 1920s excavations

Plate 33. The "Star of Tell-Ghassul": millennia-old multicolored mural

Plate 34. The pyramid linked to Joseph's waterworks, El-Fayum, Egypt

Plate 35. Remains of the subterranean "labyrinth" of Amenemhet III, El-Fayum, Egypt

Plate 36. Mount Sinai airfield in Israeli-held Sinai, 1972

Plate 37. The route of the Exodus: the Mitla Pass in the Sinai peninsula

Plate 38. In search of the real Mount Sinai: the author and the chartered airplane

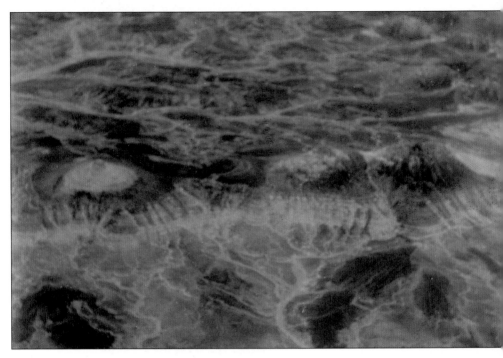

Plate 39. The UFO-like object atop Mount Sinai: aerial photograph, 1977

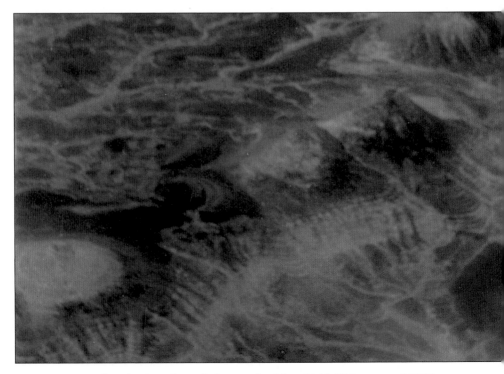

Plate 40. Second aerial photograph of the whitish "flying saucer," 1977

Plate 41. The enigmatic "landscaped feature" seen from the air, 1977

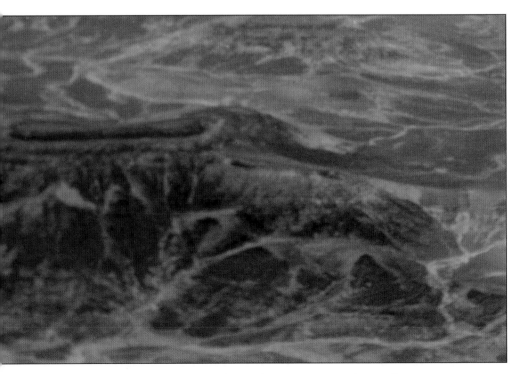

Plate 42. More Mount Sinai enigmas: the circular cave entrance, the spaced openings, 1977

Plate 43. Mount Sinai again, this time by helicopter, 1994

Plate 44. The UFO-like white feature seen again from the air, 1994

Plate 45. Second aerial photograph of the enigmatic feature, 1994

Plate 46. The bay of Ras Sudr on the Red Sea as seen from the helicopter

Plate 47 (above). Harvey, dropped off by the helicopter, stranded in the middle of nowhere

Plate 48 (left). A NASA rocket launched, streaking skyward

Plate 49. Immense stone blocks at Baalbek, Lebanon, rising ever higher

Plate 50. The colossal Trilithon in the massive western retaining wall, Baalbek

Plate 51. The immense stone block in the quarry, Baalbek

Plate 52. The Syria-Plus Expedition next to the stone block in the quarry, Baalbek

Plate 54. Technology, 700 B.C.: King Hezekiah's Water Tunnel, Jerusalem

Plate 53. "A tower whose head rises to heaven": inside the stone launch tower, Baalbek

Plate 55 (above). The tunnelers' inscription, now in the Archaeological Museum, Istanbul

Plate 56 (left). The City of David through 3,000 years: from its walls down to the spring

Plate 57 (above). The Temple Mount, Jerusalem, with the gilded Dome of the Rock

Plate 58 (left). The Western Wall today and "Robinson's Arch"

Plate 60. Pointing out one of the colossal stone blocks of the Master Course

Plate 59. In the Archaeological Tunnel: the colossal Master Course of antiquity

Plate 61. In awe of the immense stone block: the Expedition in the Tunnel

THIS POINT IS LOCATED
OPPOSITE THE
"FOUNDATION STONE"
WHICH IS THE SITE OF
THE HOLY OF HOLIES.

Plate 62. The jarring sign: You are now opposite the site of the Holy of Holies

Plate 63. The Expedition members on the Temple Mount, going up to the Dome of the Rock

Plate 64. The Foundation Rock, site of the Temple's Holy of Holies

Figure 88

Most unusually, a depiction of this Pharaoh as a sphinxlike statue shows, instead of the lion's mane, a design of fishes (fig. 88).

The accumulating evidence from antiquity pointed increasingly to Amenemhet III as the Pharaoh who had appointed Joseph, and to the Fayum and its lake as Joseph's ingenious solution to the looming problem. Further research revealed that this Pharaoh built not one but two pyramids—one near those of his father and other predecessors of the twelfth dynasty at Dahshur (see inset, fig. 89) and the other on the outskirts of the man-made lake near Hawara (see fig. 89). The latter was described by Roman historians as having next to it a "labyrinth" of countless interconnected subterranean chambers, which could have served as storage facilities.

And so it was that when the 1994 Earth Chronicles Expedition to

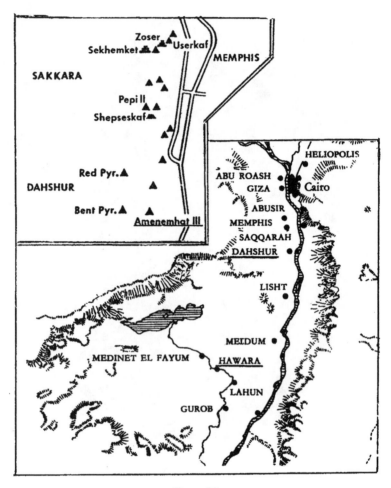

Figure 89

Egypt was planned, I set aside a full day for a visit to Dahshur and the el-Fayum areas. I had to see for myself the pyramids of Amenemhet III, the "labyrinth," the Lake, and the "Waterway of Joseph."

The planned visit was not simple to carry out. The pyramids of Dahshur, including the famed Bent Pyramid and Red Pyramid of other Middle Kingdom rulers, were located in a closed military zone. We received a special permit to enter the zone through a designated checkpoint, and for a while roamed about taking countless photographs—until a military vehicle roared upon us with an officer who furiously accused us of taking prohibited pictures of military installations (of which we could see none). He was about to jail us, confiscate our cameras and film, expel us from the area and impose other unpleasant punishments. Our able tour operator, Abbas Nadim—an Egyptian who settled in Los Angeles and operated his own tour company—managed to calm the officer down. There would be no arrests, no confiscations, but we had to climb into the tour bus and leave.

We headed, by way of some paved roads and some dirt roads that ran along or crossed irrigation canals, to the Fayum. The nearer we came, the more we left behind the desert and arid lands, and the more we could see vegetation and cultivated fields. Our target was the el-Fayum's main or central town, called Medinet ("city") el-Fayum (see fig. 89). As we neared the place, the paved road ran alongside a reasonably wide canal; we were driving alongside Bahr Yusef—the Waterway of Joseph!

In what looked like the center of town, a huge waterwheel was slowly turning, lifting, and distributing the waters brought in by the canal (fig. 90 and fig. 91). Nearby there was a restaurant with a shaded terrace—an ideal place for lunch and rest (and picture taking). I roamed about, walking along the canal, crossing and recrossing it by a footbridge. It was an exhilarating feeling: Here I was, physically verifying that a canal engineered by the Patriarch Joseph indeed existed. I was convinced that Whitehouse was correct in suggesting that Joseph was the builder of the artificial lake.

Figure 90

Figure 91

Now it was time to verify the identity of the Pharaoh of Joseph's time. It was time to proceed to the Amenemhet pyramid. But neither our tour guide nor the driver of the tour bus knew the way. Neither did the people in the restaurant; no one seemed to know the way.

Salvation appeared in the shape of a police car that came to a screeching halt near our relaxing group. The officer in charge was full of questions: Who were we, why were we here, who authorized our trip to the el-Fayum? Once again, it took some patient diplomacy by Abbas to calm the officer down. The outcome was as follows. First the bad news: We must leave and return to Cairo at once. Then the good news: The officer knew where the pyramid was and would accompany us there on the way back. Meanwhile, another police car showed up; and so, escorted by two police cars, one in front and one behind our tour bus, we drove away.

For about half an hour we drove across a fertile agricultural area; then we reached a tree line where the yellow-brown desert abruptly began. The once larger lake had shrunk down to that point, and the desert had reclaimed its own. The way now became rough and uneven. But then, in the distance, we could see a pyramidal-shaped mound rise above the plain: It was the pyramid we were looking for (plate 34). Driving through rough terrain, we came to within about a quarter of a mile from the structure;

there the officer ordered the bus stopped. You can take a few pictures from here, he said, and then you must drive away, back to Cairo!

This is nonsense, I told Abbas Nadim. The group must visit the pyramid, he told the officer. Negotiations ensued. In the end, the group was allowed to get off the bus and look around without straying away. But I, with one companion, was allowed to walk to the pyramid.

I chose Harvey H., a feature editor at a major daily newspaper in Washington, D.C., who served as an expert photographer, to come with me. As we walked toward the pyramid, we noticed that the vast field leading to it contained circular hollowings into the ground—remains of the "labyrinth" or openings to its subterranean chambers (plate 35). The pyramid was akin to some of those at Dahshur, but built of mud bricks and faced with limestones, many of which were gone. There was, to my surprise, a guard, wearing the customary long caftan. He knew a little English; I knew a little Arabic; and we were helped by the universal sign language. He confirmed that this was indeed the pyramid of Amenemhet III at Hawara. I asked if I could go in. I could not, he said, because the entrance was flooded with water.

Water? I and Harvey looked in. Indeed, after a few steps down into the pyramid's interior, one could see that it was flooded with water. But how could that be? The pyramid was some twenty miles away from the lake, several miles away even from the tree line that indicated subsurface water. Where does the water come from? I asked. *From Bahr Yusef,* the guard answered. The pyramid is linked by a subterranean channel to the Waterway of Joseph, he explained. Does the water come and go, in different seasons? I asked. No, the guard said, the water is there all the time.

That the pyramid built by the Pharaoh who had associated himself with el-Fayum was linked from its inception to the Waterway of Joseph was a true discovery, a fact unmentioned in any book on these pyramids. It was also the final proof I sought for the revolutionary idea that Joseph saved Egypt not by storing grains (which he also did, annually) but by storing water.

***

The biblical story of Joseph in Egypt forms only a chapter in the biblical history of the Hebrew Patriarchs, a link between the generations of Abraham, Isaac, and Jacob (Joseph's father) and the subsequent events of the Exodus and Moses.

As the Bible tells it, the famine that followed the seven plentiful years was widespread in the Near East, "and people from all countries came to Egypt to obtain sustenance." Among them were Jacob and his sons, the brothers of Joseph. The dramatic encounter between Joseph, grown as an Egyptian potentate and married to the daughter of the high priest of Ptah, and his brothers is recorded in the Book of Genesis (chapters 42–45); they did not recognize him but he recognized them. Forgiving his brothers for what they had done to him, Joseph told them to bring over his father too. And Jacob "and his sons and his son's sons with him, and his daughters and his son's daughters, all of his descendants, came into Egypt."

This is how the Israelites came to be in Egypt, sojourning for four centuries until a Pharaoh "who did not recall Joseph" deemed the Israelite multitude a danger, enslaved them, and started the chain of events that led to the Exodus under the leadership of Moses.

Now here is an interesting question. Moses, a Hebrew baby adopted by the Pharaoh's daughter and raised as an Egyptian prince, escaped to the Sinai after he killed an Egyptian who treated the Israelite slaves cruelly. Shepherding a flock of sheep, he wandered to the vicinity of the "Mount of the Elohim," there to hear God assign him to lead the Israelites out of bondage to the land promised to Abraham's seed. In the course of the Exodus, the Ten Commandments were granted to the Children of Israel, and the Ark of the Covenant holding the Tablets of the Law was made. So this is the question: Would all of that—great historical and religious events—not have happened if Joseph had not been sold by his brothers and taken into slavery in Egypt?

Such a "what if" question has often come up when I have been asked, How did I happen to become involved in writing about the Sumerians, the ancient civilizations, the Anunnaki, and Nibiru? The long (and true) answer which I sometimes gave was that it all began when I was a schoolboy fortunate to study the Old Testament in its original Hebrew language. The class reached chapter six of Genesis, which tells of Noah and the Deluge. The chapter begins with several very enigmatic verses, reporting that the time before the Flood was when the "giants were upon the Earth." I raised my hand and asked the teacher: Why do you say "giants" when the Hebrew word *Nefilim* means those who have come down— from heaven to Earth? Instead of being complimented on my linguistic acumen, I was reprimanded harshly: Sitchin, sit down! The teacher said, You don't question the Bible! But I was not questioning the Bible; on the contrary, I was pointing out the need to understand it accurately. Thus started my wondering who the Nefilim were, why were they cited in those verses as the sons (plural) of the Elohim (plural for "gods"). This led to the study of mythology, of ancient civilizations, of the Sumerians and their writings—and to my books.

And, more than once I was asked What If: What would have happened if the teacher, instead of reprimanding me, had complimented me? Would I have become interested in all that, would I have been led to writing my books as I did?

I, of course, do not know the answer to this What If question. But I know the answer to the What If question concerning Joseph and his brothers. When his true identity was revealed by him to his brothers, they feared for their lives for what they had done to him. But No, he said, Do not fear, for all that had happened was destined to happen. It was all part of a divine plan to send him ahead to Egypt, to make him Overseer of Egypt, to prepare food for the coming famine—all that so that when the great famine comes, his father Jacob and all his kinfolk would survive the brutal famine!

When the brothers of Joseph returned to Canaan and told Jacob their father about Joseph and his message, that they all come to Egypt, Jacob hesitated. But "Elohim appeared to Jacob in a nighttime vision" and told him: "Fear not going to Egypt, for I shall make you there into a great nation; I will go to Egypt with you, and thereafter I shall bring thee all out of there." Thus reassured, Jacob and his kinfolk went to Egypt; and as promised, when the time came, they were brought out of Egypt.

Was then my own course of events also predestined? Would there never have been a compliment instead of a reprimand—because predestination required that I be reprimanded?

Perhaps, subconsciously, that is why I went to Egypt to see the handiwork of Joseph and why I have persisted in my search for the true Mount Sinai.

***

Some postscripts:

Back in Cairo we found out that the Egyptian police were rushing tourists out of the countryside because of a terrorist alert.

Back in New York, I looked up the reports on the Hawara pyramid by the great Egyptologist Sir Flinders Petrie. He notes that the bottom of the entrance was filled with mud and water, the mud being dissolved mud bricks, but he did not dwell on the water's source. He also discovered an unusual feature in this pyramid: The inner (presumably burial) chambers are reached through hidden steps leading not deeper down, but *up* inside the pyramid—above the entrance level. To me it seems that the pyramid's builders deliberately built those secret chambers above the water level—so it must have been they who brought in the water to begin with. The Amenemhet–Joseph link was thus as old as this pyramid.

10

MOUNT SINAI MYSTERIES

This Is to Certify
That Mr./Mrs. S I T C H I N
Flew to Mount Sinai
Where Moses Received the Ten Commandments
and visited
Santa Katarina Monastery

ARKIA Israel Inland Airlines

This certificate, printed in gold lettering over a brown background, has been kept by me for some three decades in folders bulging with research materials concerning the Sinai peninsula, the Route of the Exodus, and the location of Mount Sinai. Everything stated in the certificate is true, except that the Mount to which my wife and I had gone was far from being the Mount of the Ten Commandments. In a quest to ascertain the true location of that holy mount, a series of flights and expeditions to the Sinai peninsula were undertaken; some entailed true adventures. They also resulted in photographs so incredible that I have refrained from using them in my books until now—photographs that *are now published for the first time.* These photographs pose a tantalizing challenge: Whom did Moses encounter upon the Holy Mount?

In centuries past, pilgrims to the Santa Katarina Monastery and the nearby Mount Moses, in the south of the Sinai peninsula, had to undertake a long and arduous journey to reach their destination. Going first to Egypt, most sailed down the Gulf of Suez (fig. 92) to the old port town of el-Tur, on the western coast of the peninsula, then continued, riding on donkeys, into the rugged mountainous part of the peninsula, where steep granite mountains hide the cherished peak in their midst.

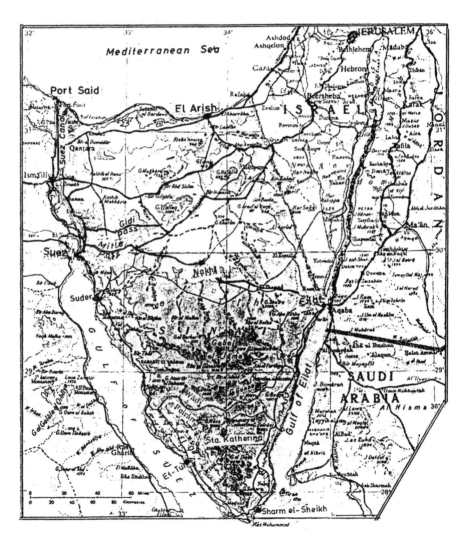

Figure 92

Figure 93

In the nineteenth century, some who went not as pilgrims but as biblical researchers (such as Johann Ludwig Burckhardt in 1816) sought to retrace the Route of the Exodus. They traveled to Suez City at the head of the Gulf of Suez, and then trekked into the peninsula proper on camelback until they reached Wadi Firan (*wadi* being a term used to denote brooks or rivulets that fill up during the rainy season and are dry beds during the rest of the year). At one place in the winding course of the wadi, nature has provided enough water to sustain a year-round oasis, the largest in the peninsula (fig. 93). A twisting and treacherous climb, many miles long, led from there on foot to the Monastery (fig. 94) and the Mount.

In the decades preceding World War I, German and British researchers (who sometimes doubled as military spies) explored the Sinai peninsula on the ground to test diverse theories regarding the location and identification of Mount Sinai (and thus establish the Route of the Exodus) or to ascertain the Route (and thus find the Mount). The Bible provides names of locations and stops en route, distances measured by days of walking, where food or water was or was not found, and other telltale details, and each theory could find support in this or that biblical

Figure 94

detail. Held by the Ottoman Turks before World War I, by the British for a while thereafter, and then by the Egyptians, the peninsula was not a welcome place for the modern descendants of the Israelites of Exodus times. But that changed when Israel captured, and held on to, the peninsula in 1967 (the Six Day War). There was an outburst of pent-up interest, and within a short time the peninsula swarmed with Israeli researchers, hikers, and sightseers.

It was thus that in 1972 my wife and I, wishing to see for ourselves the sites of the Exodus, could do that without waterless hikes or rides on the backs of donkeys. Booked on a Sinai Tour of a small Israeli airline called Arkia, we were picked up by a limousine at our hotel and delivered in time for the 8 A.M. flight from Ben-Gurion Airport to Eilat on the Gulf of Eilat. There, in a shack that was audaciously called Departure Terminal, amid young soldiers with their Uzi guns and several Hebrew-speaking Bedouins (members of local nomadic tribes that worked in Eilat's hotels), we lined up for stringent security checks, passed through a departure gate that was a door of the ex-hangar, and walked to a small airplane. We are going to fly in that? my wife asked incredulously. A few minutes later, we did.

The flight began over the breathtaking western coast of the Gulf of

Eilat, along which a newly paved highway ran to the peninsula's tip at Sharm-el-Sheikh. We were flying low to clearly see little bays, golden beaches, mountains that lipped the sea, a coral island with the remains of a Crusader fortress, and a Caliph's stronghold. To the left, the reddish mountains of Saudi Arabia were visible across the Gulf. Then the plane ascended and veered inland, striving to keep above the granite peaks that quickly began to rise ever higher, challenging the plane.

A mustached, fortyish man started to address the tourist group over the intercom, identifying the sights and landmarks below. Most everyone stood up to get a better look down. Then the seatbelt sign went on and, as in a mirage, there suddenly appeared a flat patch amidst the sharp peaks. As the plane touched down, it stopped in front of a building on which large letters announced MOUNT SINAI. It was the airstrip's terminal, the one and only building there (plate 36).

Within minutes everyone, except the tour group, had gone off in jeeps or other rough-terrain vehicles. Our bus was ready; we boarded it, and our Sinai Tour began.

The way—there is no road, just tire marks made by previous buses— wound its course southward. The flat area where the plane landed soon gave way to a path among mountain peaks that competed with each other in height, shape, and color; the path became ever steeper and nar- rower. Then the bus stopped and we were invited to get off and take a look. In a valley below one could see an oasis of date palms in the dis- tance: the oasis of Wadi Firan.

Resuming the journey over increasingly rugged terrain, the panorama continued to be one of barren mountains, with not a soul in sight. The bus creaked as it made its way slowly on a rocky path cleared between boulders that had rolled down the cliffs. Then a sharp descent began and an unexpected tranquil valley appeared. There, in the midst of the moun- tains, stood what looked like a medieval castle surrounded by walls: the monastery of Santa Katarina.

After a precarious descent, the bus reached the outskirts of the monastery. In years past the only way in was to be hauled up in a basket. We entered more easily, through a gate adjoining the monks' vegetable and fruit garden. A monk whose task it was to welcome visitors explained that the history of the place goes back to the beginning of Christianity, when early converts in Egypt (then under Roman rule) escaped to the deserts, in Egypt and the Sinai, to avoid persecution; numerous hideouts evolved into monasteries after the emperor Constantine recognized

Christianity as the state religion. Among the martyrs executed by the Romans was one called Katherine; angels snatched her body and hid it upon the Sinai's highest peak. Four centuries later, her burial place was revealed to a monk in a dream. The mount and the monastery near it thus bear her name. A tour of the church, the library, and the spot where the golden casket of Saint Catherine is kept, followed.

But, we asked, what about Mount Sinai?

Outside, the tour guide pointed to a distant peak (fig. 95); it is not called Mount Sinai but Jebel Mussa, the Mount of Moses. Situated about two hours' walk from the monastery, it is not a stand-alone mount but the southern peak of a two-mile-long massif. It can be reached in two ways, the guide explained. One way entails climbing up 4,000 steps laid out by the monks along the western slopes of the massif. Another, easier but longer way leads gradually up the eastern slopes of the massif until it connects with the last 750 steps of the western way.

Those who wished to climb up had to reserve overnight accommodations at the monastery, then rise at dawn to start the climbs up and down. Others (my wife and me included) who had made no such reservations were taken back by the bus to the airstrip, for a short flight for a

Figure 95

side tour to Sharm-el-Sheikh at the peninsula's tip; there the Israelis developed a beach resort, naming it Ophirah—To Ophir—pointing the way to the fabulous land where, according to the Bible, Solomon obtained the gold for the Temple in Jerusalem.

Our visit to the monastery had established that the Moses (Mussa in Arabic) after whom Mount Moses was named was not at all Moses of the Exodus, but a monk who was involved in finding Saint Catherine's body. It made clear that Mount Mussa was not a mount at all, but the end peak of a two-mile-long massif, and that around it there were mountain peaks (including Mount Katherine itself, as a sign in the monastery proclaimed) that rose higher, belittling, as it were, God's choice of a peak on which to make an appearance (fig. 96). And furthermore, not being a stand-alone mount, it could in no way meet the biblical description of the Israelites encamped all around the mount.

In winter, the high granite peaks are snow-covered; there is no mention of snowfall at all in the biblical narrative of the Exodus. Indeed, the mount where Moses saw the first miracle, that of the Burning Bush that

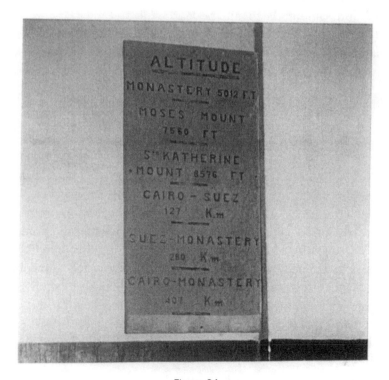

Figure 96

was not consumed, is called in the Bible Mount *Horeb,* the Mount in the Dryness. The oasis of Firan, assuming that it was the source of water to the Israelites (600,000 of them!), is several miles away from Mount Moses of the monks; if the Israelites were encamped there, at the oasis, there is no way they could have witnessed the Great Theophany of Mount Sinai "where Yahweh came down upon Mount Sinai" (Exodus 19:20).

And then there was the matter of the quails. Miraculously, when the Israelites ran out of food, quails by the thousands landed near the encampment. The birds were so exhausted that they could just be picked up. Now, quails do fly over the Sinai to this day—migrating in winter from Romania and the Black Sea lands to Africa, in the Sudan, and returning in springtime. But they do not fly over the southern part of the Sinai, because the peaks are much too high for them. They fly over the central-northern part of the peninsula, and come to rest on the way back in that part of the peninsula before undertaking the long, uninterrupted flight over the Mediterranean Sea. They do that at exactly the time indicated in the Exodus story, at Passover time, when spring begins, but not in the south, among the granite peaks.

If anything, the trip convinced me that the Mount Moses near the monastery was not, as the certificate claimed, the mount "where Moses received the Ten Commandments."

✳✳✳

At the time of that 1972 trip I was writing *The 12th Planet,* stopping to do more research when an aspect of the book called for additional verification. The location of Mount Sinai, the true Mount Sinai, was important because one of its principal names in the Bible is Har Ha-Elohim, translated Mount of God, but literally meaning "the Mount of the gods," plural. The term *Elohim* is used in Genesis to describe the group that said, "Let us fashion the Adam in our image and after our likeness." Contrary to accepted wisdom, I concluded that the parallel (and earlier) Mesopotamian texts indicated that the Elohim, literally the Lofty Ones, were one and the same as the *Anunnaki*—those who from heaven to Earth came, the gods of the Sumerians and of the Babylonians and Assyrians and Egyptians and all other peoples who followed them in antiquity.

Among the literary texts bequeathed to us by the Sumerians is the

Epic of Gilgamesh, the king of Uruk (the biblical Erech), who, being of two-thirds Anunnaki descent, went in search of immortality. His first journey was to the Landing Place in the Cedar Mountain (the subject of another chapter in this book). Having failed there, he tried again at the place where the Anunnaki had their spaceport. That place was, I concluded, in the Sinai peninsula, near the mountain called in the Sumerian text Mount *Mashu* (sounding so much like Mount of *Moshe,* the Hebrew name of Moses). That it was one and the same as the Mount of the Elohim seemed very plausible. So, locating the real Mount Sinai could tie together many pieces of evidence regarding the Anunnaki.

The spaceport to which Gilgamesh had gone was the one established by the Anunnaki after the Deluge (an earlier one, in the Land Between the Rivers, perished and was buried under millions of tons of mud). I had hoped that the tour of the Sinai described above would provide the missing link in the chain of evidence, but the conclusion that the "traditional" Mount Sinai near the monastery was not the correct one was one thing; to find the true mount was still an unfinished task. And so *The 12th Planet* ended with the Deluge, leaving for the next book the tales of the second spaceport and Gilgamesh.

In researching and writing, writing and researching that next book, *The Stairway to Heaven,* I set aside the biblical investigation and focused instead on the Sumerian data on the one hand and the Egyptian data on the other hand. Gilgamesh, coming from the east, and Egyptian Pharaohs in their quest for eternal Afterlife coming from the west, both appeared to be converging on a single similar geographic point. Their identical target was the Sinai peninsula. But where in the peninsula?

As is more fully explained and illustrated in *The Stairway to Heaven,* the destination of Gilgamesh's second journey was the post-Diluvial spaceport, whose Landing Corridor, Mission Control Center, and other connecting lines converged in the peninsula's central plain (fig. 97). The Pharaohs' Afterlife journey took them along a sightline that I named The Gaze of the Sphinx, a line that ran along the 30th parallel north (the dotted line on the map). Where the landing line and the 30th parallel intersected—there, I concluded, the spaceport had to be (the point marked SP on the map). And both Sumerian and Egyptian texts spoke of a mount with subterranean facilities that was located beside the landing place. It was only logical that in the Bible that Mount would be referred to as the Mount of the Elohim.

Studying practically every report in English, German, and French by

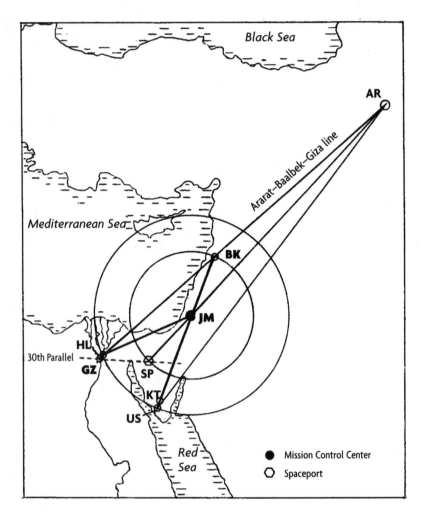

Figure 97

archaeologists and military men regarding Mount Sinai and the Route of the Exodus, it was clear that ever since the Burckhardt report threw doubt on the mount near the monastery, virtually everyone had discarded the southern route and location and opted for either a northern one (closer to the Mediterranean Sea, the route called by the Romans Via Maris) or a central location and route, known variously as the Route of the Patriarchs or the Way of Shur. The majority of them opted for the central location. But the Sinai's central plain is surrounded by a chain of mountains—not a tight continuous one, but one with small and large gaps. Which one of those mountains was *the* one? There, scholarly opinions differed.

My files remind me how extensive was my correspondence with the Israeli researchers, the Israel Exploration Society (of which I have been a member), the Hebrew University in Jerusalem, and the Tel-Aviv University, during the years 1973–1975, in regard to their candidate for Mount Sinai. The result was a firm conviction on my part as to which mount was the one; it was one that not only fitted the others' multiple choices (based on the biblical narrative, geography and topography, climate, water resources, etc.); it also had to fit *my* spaceport and landing-corridor maps.

But when my mind was made up and I was writing so in the second book's manuscript, I was one day seized with panic. The spacecraft of the Anunnaki, I presumed, descended down the central line in the Landing Corridor, that was anchored on the twin peaks of Ararat, passed over Mission Control Center (Jerusalem), and glided down to a touchdown at the spaceport (see fig. 97, page 138). But what if, it suddenly dawned on me, right there as the craft was low enough to glide down, one of the mountains reared its ugly head? Instead of a landing there would be a crashing. And, if my book is published as I have been writing it and someone could come and say: Nonsense, there's a high mountain there in the way! I would look stupid, and rightly so.

And so, as soon as *The 12th Planet* was published in 1976, I armed myself with all the pull and introductions I could muster and went with my wife to Israel again. My mission this time was to arrange a flight that would simulate the descent of an Anunnaki spacecraft, to see for myself if my theory and diagrams were feasible (or not).

Through contacts it appeared that the only way to accomplish my mission would be via a private flight in a chartered plane; I agreed to bear the high cost. But that was only the beginning. In order to fly there, a flight plan had to be presented to and authorized by the military authorities who controlled the airspace. How far into the Sinai did I wish to fly, what did I want to see, and why? When I categorized my purpose as "archaeological," I was told that I must have the approval of the Chief Military Archaeologist for Northern Sinai.

His name is recorded in my notes from the time: Dov Meron. We met at his home in Ashkelon, on the Mediterranean coast north of Gaza. He proved well versed in all aspects of the Sinai peninsula—topography, climate, water resources, history. We started with my ideas on the Route

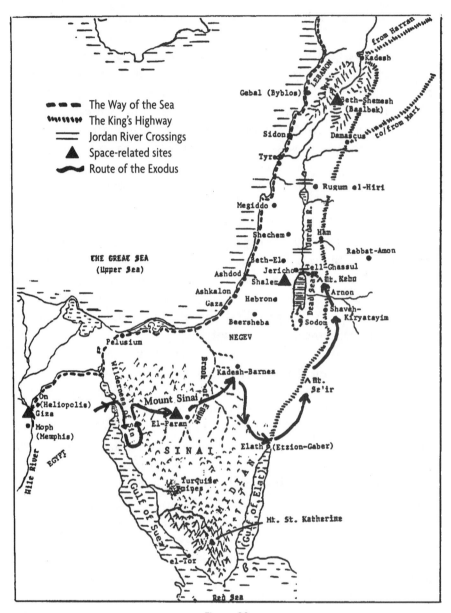

Figure 98

of the Exodus (fig. 98) and my conclusion that the Israelites entered the central plain through the pass now called Mitla Pass, where battles in the 1967 Israeli-Egyptian war proved crucial (plate 37); I told him that I would like to overfly the Mitla Pass and the alternative Giddi Pass.

Then we came around to the subject of Mount Sinai itself and its possible location. I reviewed for him the pros and cons of other researchers, with arguments converging on the central plain. And then I decided to put my cards on the table. I pulled out from my briefcase a copy of the newly published *The 12th Planet* and explained to him the "Anunnaki connection." He was fascinated rather than shocked. There is one mountain that meets all these criteria, he said, and pointed it out on the large Sinai map in front of us.

It was the very same mountain to which my own research had pointed!

Right then and there, in my presence, he prepared the written approval and recommendation that I be allowed to fly to the Mount and the passes. I was tickled pink.

Taking it from there through the military chain of approvals, it turned out that naming the mountain caused a problem. Since it was located south-southwest of the town of el-Arish (see map, fig. 92, page 130), the approved route called for flying south over the Mediterranean Sea and turning inland, to the Sinai proper, only at el-Arish. But that was not good for my initial purpose: to verify the viability of the Landing Path of the Anunnaki. No, we had to fly to and turn south *from Jerusalem,* I insisted. In the end, I was allowed to fly that way, but had to start somewhat south of Jerusalem.

With one problem solved, others cropped up, among them my desire to take photographs. I got an OK providing I shoot no more than two rolls of film and hand them over to the army liaison officer who would accompany me, for the army to develop and censor out whatever shouldn't be photographed. I had no choice but to agree.

It was a pleasant autumn day in November 1977 when we took off from Sdeh Dov, a small civilian airfield north of Tel-Aviv. I asked the liaison officer, before boarding, to take a picture of me by the plane—and here it is (plate 38). I and he were the only passengers in the seventeen-seat plane; the pilot was assigned by the Israeli air force. South of Jerusalem we turned south, to follow the Path of the Anunnaki. Even from the moderate altitude, the narrowness of Israel was there to be seen; it seemed that if one stretched a hand out from this side, the Mediterranean would be touched, and from the other side, the Jordan River and the Dead Sea.

We flew now straight south, gradually reducing the altitude. The mountains of Judea began to give way to a terrain of rolling hills. Then, right ahead of us, the hills became ominous mountains. Keep going lower! Keep going lower! I shouted to the worried pilot, unsure myself whether we would have to "chicken out"and either veer off course or climb higher. But then, as if by magic, the mountains parted and there was a gap, a very wide gap in the mountain chain. We passed through the breach as though a giant hand had snatched the mountains to our left and right and pulled them away; and ahead of us, the Sinai's central plain came into full view.

Our altitude was about 2,000 feet. I could hear the pilot sigh with relief (or so I think I heard). We're OK! We're OK! I cried out loud; You can resume normal altitude now, I said to the pilot.

A great feeling of "I did it!" swept over me. I took out a bottle of wine (that I brought along "just in case") and cookies, and invited my companions to share my joy: I had followed the Landing Path of the Anunnaki, and ascertained its feasibility! The liaison officer shared the wine and cookies; the pilot just the cookies.

***

We now continued westward, flying over the Sinai's central plain. Below, the carcasses of tanks and other vehicles of war could still be seen, remnants from the 1973 Sinai Egyptian–Israeli war—the hard soil of the plain, military commentators wrote, was "perfect tank terrain." Burnt trucks marked out old roads; new roads ran through the terrain as black asphalt ribbons. We flew toward the Mitla and Giddi Passes only as far as the armistice lines permitted, then turned back. Our reference point was the habitat ("town" would be an exaggeration) of Nakhl, a crossroads astride the Sinai's main tributary, Wadi el-Arish.

It had rained the night before, and the Wadi overflowed with water, so much so that at some points small lakes formed. Besides rainfall in the winter season, the Wadi is also fed with water flowing off the southern peaks as their snows melt in the spring. Even in the dry summer season, there is water just a few inches below the dry riverbed. If the Israelites encamped there—as I believe—it would explain why once they arrived there they had water for themselves and for their flocks. It would also explain the incident of the Golden Calf, which Moses "ground into powder and strew . . . upon the water, and made the Children of Israel drink thereof."

As a prominent peak, the Mount of the Exodus—Mount Mashu of the Gilgamesh epic—had to be on the perimeter of the spaceport, not in its midst (otherwise the craft would crash into it). As we approached

Nakhl and viewed the white limestone chain of mountains surrounding the plain, I pointed out to the pilot on my Sinai map the particular mountain to which I wished to go.

It stood alone; the Israelites, encamped all around it as the Bible described, would have had no problem seeing whatever was happening upon the Mount—the fiery landing of the Lord in his *Kavod* upon the Mount. Though usually translated "glory," the term literally meant in the Semitic languages "the heavy thing" (and, if a Sumerian term, meant "that which soars"). The Israelites had seen it when they entered the desert leading to the Mount, and were told that they would see it again when the Lord spoke to Moses from the Mount so that all the people would know that he carried the words of God to them. Given three days' notice, the people experienced the greatest theophany ever, when the Lord in his *Kavod* landed on the Mount within a heavy cloud. "And the appearance of the *Kavod* of Yahweh was like a devouring fire on the top of the Mount, visible to the children of Israel; And Moses went into the cloud, and ascended the Mount, and was upon the Mount forty days and forty nights" (according to the Book of Exodus).

That was some 3,400 years ago. And now I, belonging to the same Hebrew tribe as Moses and Aaron—the Levites—was about to revisit that awesome and sacred site, seeing it not from the foot of the Mount as the Israelite multitude did, but from its top!

Was I expecting to find any ancient remains on the Mount, remnants from that unique time when the people saw the Lord and heard him speak to Moses? Of course not (at least, that's what logic told me . . .). Those events connected with the Ten Commandments occurred and passed, leaving nothing behind. What I thought might be found was a *cave* or a cavelike feature. The only time the Bible speaks of Mount Sinai again in post-Exodus times is in the tale of the Prophet Elijah. After he had caused the slaying of the priests of Ba'al, he escaped for his life to the Sinai. There an angel led him to a cave on Mount Sinai, where he could take refuge. A cave, I thought, might remain even after thousands of years; maybe I would see it?

We circled the mountain several times, but I saw nothing of interest. I then asked the pilot to fly over the mountain and crisscross it a few times. I took a few snapshots of the terrain on top of the mountain, to have a photographic record. The weather was changing; it was getting cloudy and windy. The pilot suggested that we turn back home. I had some film left; let's crisscross the mountaintop once more, I said. There seemed to be some topographic features that had a "manicured" or land-scaped look to them.

Obliging, the pilot made a full circle and began another run across the mountaintop. I directed him toward a kind of promontory or rise that stood out, oddly shaped as if on purpose. As we neared it, there seemed to be a circular opening on its side. My pulse quickened: Had I found the cave? I took a couple of snapshots and asked the pilot to circle again so as to have a look at this feature from its other side.

He did, and it was then that my eye caught a bright, white, round feature that stood out from the rest of the gray-brown landscape. I managed to shoot it with my camera a couple of times (plates 39 and 40), wondering what it was. And then I saw that I had reached the end of the film—the second roll of my allowance.

"We must return!" the pilot said. "We might as well," I said. "I am out of film."

As required, I handed over the two black-and-white films to the liaison officer. He promised they would be developed and looked over by the military "right away." I ended up waiting several days, literally until I had to leave for the airport to fly back to New York. I opened the sealed envelope on the plane and saw on the contact sheets that several photos were obliterated (though I had been careful not to shoot anything that looked like a military installation).

Back in New York, I rushed to have the film printed and enlarged. *The white object showed up as I have seen it from the air: perfectly circular, exactly as flying saucers have been described by those who claim to have seen them, with a protruding top.* If I were to draw a UFO, that is how I would have depicted it!

If that was not quite incredible, no less amazing were the details captured in the photographs of the "cave" and "landscaped feature" (plate 41) and the perfectly circular "cave" opening (plate 42). The promontory that had caught my attention, shot from one side from above it (plate 41), was actually divided into two parts, one extending like a long tongue and the other as an oblong area around which the ground was ploughed so that the central portion rose above its ground level. Seen from the other side where the "cave" attracted my attention to begin with, the photograph (plate 42) did indeed show a perfectly circular cavity in the side of the promontory. *But more astonishingly, the rise above it had a series of openings on top, equally spaced. The photograph clearly showed three such openings and perhaps a fourth one* (on the left at the picture's edge).

Beyond these openings, at the topmost part of this rise, the "ploughed" oblong portion appeared as a long feature, darker (in the black-and-white photograph) than its surroundings.

I looked at these photographs over and over again. Further enlargements blurred rather than improved the images. It was all too incredible, yet there it was. I asked myself question after question, nodding my head in disbelief, for none of the answers seemed plausible. Did I just happen to fly over the Mount while a UFO—a modern UFO—had landed upon it? Did I come upon an object that has been there for a while? And, most impossible of all, did I see and take a picture of the divine *Kavod* remaining there from the time of the Exodus or from another return visit by Yahweh? Or, less astounding but more logical, was it after all a natural feature, carved out by rain and wind, white because it was an exposed part of the limestone mountain?

And what about the other odd features—the "manicured" or ploughed-around elevated promontory, the perfectly circular "cave entrance," the evenly spaced openings—what could they be? Surely, all that could not be the work of rain and wind. This was the engineered handiwork of *someone*—if not men, then gods.

Egyptian texts describing the Pharaoh's Journey in the Afterlife, from his burial place to the *Duat* where the Mountain of Light was situated, conceived of it as a twelve-hour journey. Journeying above ground for the first three hours, the king entered an opening leading down via a series of sloping tunnels, reaching the lowest level in the Fifth Hour. In the Sixth Hour he was judged as to whether he was worthy of joining the gods on their Planet of Millions of Years; and if found worthy, he proceeded along tunnels sloping upward (fig. 99) via a gateway that bore the emblem of the Winged Disc. In the Twelfth Hour he reached "the outermost limit of thick darkness," where in a large cavern the Ascender to Heaven was awaiting him; and there, attired for the journey, "the Door of Earth, the Door to Heaven" opened, and he was carried aloft.

Looking again at my photographs, I wondered whether the odd feature with its series of spaced apertures represents the openings of air shafts to subterranean facilities within the mountain, as described in the Egyptian texts and *Book of the Dead* depictions. Was the circular cavelike entrance the "cleft" where Moses was instructed to hide when the Lord passed by him on the mount, or was it the cave where Elijah hid—an opening also connected to some passages inside the mount?

As these thoughts raced through my mind, I also could not help but

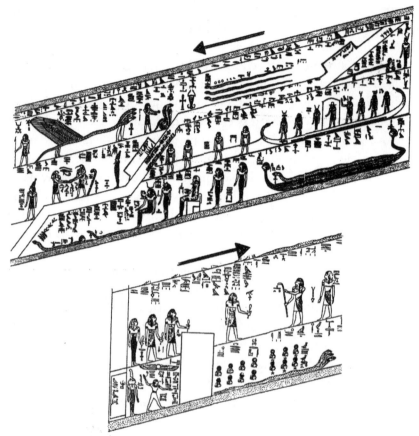

Figure 99

wonder whether these features too were somehow the product of natural forces, or even illusions of rock formations and the play of light and shadow. And speaking of illusions, I could not take my eyes (and my magnifying glass) away from what *looked like a giant wearing armor standing beside the cave entrance.* As crazy as that sounds, that is how it looked.

It was all incredible, mind-boggling, impossible, too good to be true. If true, then I had come upon and photographed physical evidence of Anunnaki presences upon the mount—and confirmation of their spaceport, which had to be located nearby, a spaceport that was wiped out in a nuclear encounter that the Bible recalls as the upheaval of Sodom and Gomorrah. On the other hand, if not true, then nature conspired to create a most amazing set of enigmatic features—an amazing sight in itself.

Which was it?

I felt that this was too important to be left without further investigation. It was necessary, I felt, to get back to the Mount and land on top, to physically check out these amazing features. And since I was not a candidate for mountain climbing, I had to get there by helicopter.

Events forced me to act more quickly than I would have liked. In March 1979 the terms of an Israeli-Egyptian peace agreement were revealed, which called for Israeli withdrawal from the Sinai in stages—and the area where "my" mount was located had to be evacuated by December of that year (fig. 100).

Hurriedly, I flew back to Israel, to obtain a helicopter and permission to land on the Mount. I hit a brick wall: All planes and helicopters, even

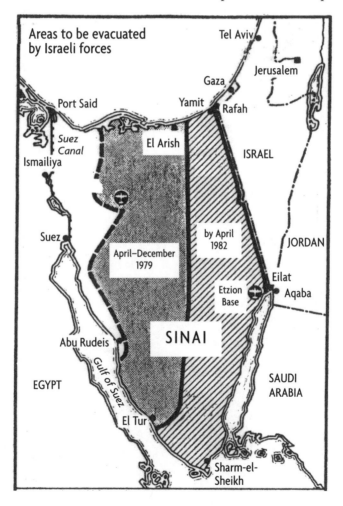

Figure 100

those used for crop dusting, were mobilized for the removal of equipment from the Sinai. All non-essential flights, tours, whatever was not connected with the dismantling of army and air force bases, were banned. I spent more than a week in futile efforts, then gave up.

Back home, I was finishing writing and illustrating *The Stairway to Heaven* (which was published in 1980). I decided that, as a responsible researcher, I could not include the incredible findings or show the photographs without the on-the-spot verification. And so it was that *The Stairway to Heaven* went to print without the photos and without the tale of my 1977 flight. *The photos shown here have been kept by me unpublished for a quarter of a century!*

But I did not give up trying to get back to the Mount, with a helicopter; the saga of the Mount Sinai Mysteries had to be continued.

11

THE ELUSIVE MOUNT ADVENTURES

The self-imposed need to attain on-the-spot verification of the puzzling features atop the Mount Sinai of my choice led, in time, to most unexpected consequences and adventures. And, for about two decades, my efforts repeatedly ran into international power politics—affairs of state with which I sought no connection (but became enmeshed in anyway).

My air trips to the Sinai peninsula, as described, were in themselves made possible because of the Israeli-Egyptian war of 1967. My hurried return to Israel to obtain a helicopter for landing upon the Mount in 1979 was prompted by the unfolding peace process between Egypt and Israel and the Peace Treaty requirements for a staged evacuation of the Sinai peninsula by the Israelis.

What I did not know at that time was that while I was in Israel trying to obtain a helicopter to go to Mount Sinai, there was someone else—in Egypt—who was planning a helicopter flight to Mount Sinai. That someone was none other than Anwar Sadat, the President of Egypt! His plans, however, focused on Mount Mussa near the St. Catherine monastery, the so-called traditional Mount Sinai. Yet his intentions, and his helicopter flight, did play a part in my own subsequent plans and Expeditions.

As it turned out, President Sadat of Egypt envisioned the historical signing of the Egyptian-Israeli Peace Treaty as an occasion for a unique ecumenical event. He proposed that he, Prime Minister Menachem Begin of Israel, and President Jimmy Carter of the United States—a Moslem, a Jew, and a Christian—come to the Sinai and hold the treaty-signing ceremony at the foot of "Mount Sinai, where God gave Moses the Ten Commandments." The ceremony took place, instead, on the lawn of the White House in Washington (in March 1979). But as a gesture of goodwill, Israel agreed to adjust the line of withdrawal required by December 1979 so that the Mount and the monastery would be handed over to the Egyptians by the earlier signing date rather than by April 1982. And so it was that no sooner did the Israelis leave than the Egyptians, on Sadat's personal orders, began the construction of an Interfaith House of Worship near the monastery, as part of a planned Peace Village.

President Sadat flew in by helicopter to conduct the ceremonies in person.

And when I learned of it, I thought to myself: Hey, maybe I could interest Sadat in my searches and persuade him to provide me with a helicopter?

As outlandish as the idea might seem, I did follow it up. As soon as *The Stairway to Heaven* was published, the publisher, St. Martin's Press, sent a copy to President Sadat; the accompanying letter (signed by Thomas L. Dunne, Executive Editor) stressed my theories "concerning the Pyramids and the Search for Immortality." Whether the book ever reached Sadat I don't know, but there was no answer.

Not giving the idea up, I found another avenue to reach Sadat. Among the fans that I had acquired after publication of *The 12th Planet* was one who knew the Egyptian Ambassador in Washington, His Excellency Ashraf A. Ghorbal. At my request he sent the Ambassador two copies of my new book, *The Stairway to Heaven,* one for the Ambassador and one to be forwarded to President Sadat. The purpose was clearly stated, "Mr. Sitchin," my fan wrote to the Ambassador, "has a great ambition to go by helicopter to a certain mountain in the area of Nakhl."

The Ambassador in acknowledgment assured us that the book and the request would be sent to President Sadat in Cairo. Whether President Sadat did receive the book and the request became moot when he was assassinated, in October 1981, by Islamic fanatics opposed to the Peace Treaty with Israel.

What now? As April 1982 arrived and the Sinai peninsula was fully handed over to the Egyptians, it was clear to me that henceforth the only way to reach the Mount would be through Egypt; if not by starting at the very top, then by more conventional methods. I got in touch with travel and tour agencies specializing in travel to Egypt. Private tours to the Sinai were not allowed yet, I was told; it was a military zone, and entry was allowed by special permit only.

I had been a member of the Israel Exploration Society from long ago; now I joined as a member the American Research Center in Egypt (ARCE), hoping to get assistance through them. At one of their meetings in New York I was introduced to Dr. Mohamed Ibrahim Bakr, Chairman of the Egyptian Antiquities Organization; he promised his help, but nothing came of it. The Director of ARCE in Cairo made inquiries; in the end, he suggested that I come to Cairo and personally try to get the helicopter permit. To ensure that such a trip would be successful, I armed myself with a variety of letters of recommendation. One of them was to a former minister in Sadat's government who was sitting behind Sadat on the reviewing stand when the assassination took place. Another was from Dr. Zahi Hawass (then Chief Inspector of the Giza Pyramids and in time the supreme authority thereof as Director General), who was then spending time at the University Museum in Philadelphia and has read *The 12th Planet* and *The Stairway to Heaven*.

The trip, after all those extensive preparations, took place in early November 1984—seven years, almost to the day, after my memorable flight to the Mount. When I arrived in Cairo with my wife, we were made welcome by all with whom I had been in touch; everyone promised to help us get the helicopter permit "for archaeological research." While waiting for their efforts to reach fruition, we toured whatever is toured in Egypt traditionally. But those trying to pull strings on my behalf were told that my destination, a mountain in central Sinai, was not on the archaeological list. They were advised to get the support of the Minister of Culture, but he was away.

Unable to continue staying in Cairo, I returned to New York and continued my efforts from there, without success. I was back in Cairo several more times between then and 1992, researching for my continued writings as well as trying to attain a breakthrough. By the time I returned in 1992, the Egyptians had relaxed the restrictions on travel to the peninsula, and had even picked up where the Israelis left off in the development of tourist resorts in the Sinai. There was even a hint that a permit for a helicopter flight might be issued. There was only one problem: Only the military was allowed to fly over the Sinai due to certain restrictions imposed on military forces by the terms of the Peace Treaty with Israel (or so I was told).

The 1992 visit, it turned out later, was a trigger to an eventual helicopter flight. In the course of that visit I gave a lecture at the Mena House Hotel—situated next to the Giza pyramids and venue of Egyptian-Israeli peace negotiations—at an international conference arranged by an outfit called Power Places Tours. Stealing into the conference hall was a competitor of theirs—Abbas Nadim, an Egyptian tourism expert who moved to the United States and formed his own company, Visions Travel & Tours. He contacted me when we were both back in the United States and invited me to join some of his tours and conferences. I said that what I was really interested in was to have my own special tours, to places selected by me, open to participation by people who have read my books.

No problem, he said; where do you want to go? I have the best contacts in Egypt. To the Sinai, I said. I can arrange all-terrain vehicles, he said. That's good, I said, but I also need a helicopter . . . He promised to investigate. I knew that nothing would come of it, as none were privately available for Sinai flights. Then, to my utter surprise, Abbas Nadim called me and said: I can get you a helicopter!

The outcome was a plan to visit certain sites in Egypt—the "must-

Figure 101

see" ones plus others of my choice—and then go into the Sinai peninsula. The tour was named IN THE FOOTSTEPS OF THE EXODUS, and was to coincide with the time of the Exodus, springtime. We were to reach Nakhl, in the central plain, by tour bus. There, a helicopter would await me and would take me to the Mount as I wished.

It was spring 1994. An enthusiastic group of Sitchin fans signed on. We toured the Cairo Museum, the Giza pyramids, other pyramids, the el-Fayum oasis, Karnak, Luxor, the Valley of the Kings. Abbas Nadim kept assuring me that all was well regarding the helicopter. Back in Cairo, I overheard him engaged in frantic phone calls. Is there any problem with the helicopter? I asked worriedly. No, no, no! he said, everything will be OK.

On the designated day we took off in our tour bus to the Sinai. We were told that we were the first tour group in a civilian bus allowed to reach the Sinai, not via the regular bridges over the Suez Canal, but via the tunnel that the Egyptians had secretly built, under the Canal, when they prepared their attack on the Israeli positions in 1973 (fig. 101). It was a bittersweet experience for me that continued as we were allowed, once through the Canal Tunnel with a military escort, to turn back and visit the ruins of the former Israeli defense positions on the Canal's eastern bank, known as the Bar-Lev Line (fig. 102). One of the participants in the tour, a young woman named Shoshana, had been a soldier in the

Figure 102

Israeli Army stationed right there. I joined the tour, she said, to see this place again.

The place was testimony to a bitter past; that she could revisit it under Egyptian auspices was, one hoped, an augury of better times. Such sentiments followed me (and her) as we drove through the famed Mitla Pass, a scene of fierce battles in the recent past as well as during the Exodus. Burnt and destroyed military vehicles still lined the pass, though not as many as aerial photographs from the battle time showed (fig. 103). Almost everywhere along the road through the pass there were still signs warning: DANGER—LANDMINES.

Several hours after leaving Cairo, we reached Nakhl (or Nakhla, as the Egyptians called it). Unlike the place that I saw from the air in 1977, it was more like a town, with camels and donkeys roaming its dusty streets alongside cars. We stopped at a nondescript building at the edge of a market square—the town's restaurant, our driver said. We were hungry, thirsty, and tired, and ready for a good meal. The safe choices were pita (flatbread), cheese, and hardboiled eggs, with sweet tea or bottled soft drinks cooled by floating in a tank of water.

Where is the helicopter? I demanded to know from Abbas. It's coming, it's coming, he assured me; in the meantime, have something to eat.

I asked one of the group's members, Harvey Hagman—who was a feature editor at the *Washington Times* and had brought along a video camera—to sit near me. I revealed to him, under strict secrecy, that I was about to board a helicopter to fly to and land on a nearby mountain while the group was having the lunch break. I told him that I expected to see some interesting features on the mountain, which I considered to be the real Mount Sinai; and I wanted him to come along, as a witness. He readily agreed.

About fifteen minutes into the stop Abbas burst into the place and shouted to me: Come quick! Come quick! The taxi is waiting! I rushed out after him, accompanied by Harvey. What taxi? I shouted to Abbas.

The helicopter cannot come to Nakhla, he said. They sent the taxi to bring us to the helicopter.

Still holding on to the pita and cheese, I joined Harvey and Abbas in the taxi—an aged car with a driver in front. I sat beside the driver and the other two sat in the back. The taxi headed south on an asphalt road on which we were the only car, in either direction. Abbas and the driver exchanged words in Arabic. We are late; I hope we make it, Abbas said. I gave him a nasty look. The driver raised speed—I saw the speedometer

Figure 103

needle at the edge of its maximum; it felt as if the car was airborne, not touching the road. The drive went on and on. Are you sure we are going to some helicopter? I asked Abbas.

It was about then that we suddenly saw in the distance what looked like an airfield and a helicopter parked there. The taxi made a few turns and arrived on the tarmac beside the helicopter. I wanted to have a picture taken of me beside the helicopter, like the one I had taken beside the plane in Tel-Aviv seventeen years earlier. "No pictures! No pictures!" a middle-aged man standing beside the helicopter shouted. "Quick, we must leave!" he continued in English, "it is very late!"

The pilot was already seated in the helicopter. I went in and sat beside him. The other three—Abbas, Harvey, and the unidentified man—sat in the back. The pilot introduced himself to me in English, giving his first name, a German name. He handed me a helmet with earphones. Because of the propeller noise, he said, we can talk to each other only via these earphones. He asked me to show him our destination on his air map. I pointed it out, and we took off.

It was my first flight in a helicopter, and it was quite different from flying in an airplane, of any size. You not only feel but you actually can see that there is nothing under you, that somehow you are pendant in the air and could drop down if an unseen force stops holding you up . . . The unease prevented me from enjoying the thrill of seeing the cherished Sinai from such a vantage point; thankfully the flight to our destination was not a long one. We passed over Nakhl and its main square, low enough to see people, vehicles, camels; I did not see our bus. I turned back and gestured a question mark to Abbas, but he waved his hands to show OK, OK.

The pilot wanted to know where to go now, and it wasn't easy to direct him because things look different from high above than on a flat map. I fished out my own maps, and indicated the Mount to him. After a few minutes of flying, I pointed out the Mount with my hands. Get lower, and fly along its circumference, I told the pilot. I was hoping that I would recognize the curving contours that my erstwhile photographs show from when we made the run toward the bright feature, seventeen years ago. I wondered whether we could locate the spot, whether the bright object would still be there. What if it's gone, I thought to myself, and the confirmation I was seeking was not there anymore? Then it occurred to me that if the bright object were gone, Wow! It would prove that it was a UFO that had landed and took off! But what if I just don't locate it? Now two (or three) witnesses would testify that there was nothing there . . .

But this speculation came to an abrupt end as I saw the UFO-like feature. There it is! I shouted to the pilot, as I quickly took several pictures (plates 43, 44, and 45). I pointed it out to the people in the back, who could not hear my words.

"Come down there!" I shouted to the pilot. "Land beside it!"

He gave me a puzzled look. "No landing, no time!" he shouted back.

I took off my helmet with its earphones and turned to Abbas in the back. "The pilot refuses to come down, to land!" I shouted to him. "We must touch down!"

The unidentified man could also hear me. He looked at his watch, spoke in Arabic to Abbas, quite agitated. "It cannot be done!" Abbas shouted to me. "We must do it!" I shouted back. But I was straining my voice in vain. The pilot had already turned the helicopter, and we were off the mountaintop, flying away.

I was bursting with anger. "What the hell is going on?!" I shouted to Abbas. He leaned forward so that I could hear him. "The helicopter is expected at Ras Sudr by a certain time," he shouted. "There is no time left; I will explain, Zecharia, I will explain!"

Ras Sudr, I knew, was a sleepy village on the Sinai's Red Sea coast that became the center of oil-drilling activities after the Israelis found oil off the Sinai's coast. Drilling platforms were erected offshore, the oil was piped to the coast, and a small harbor was developed for small tankers to carry off the crude oil. The Egyptians, with help from European oil companies, kept the operations going. Ras Sudr—the village, not the oil-workers camp (see map, fig. 92, page 130)—was where our group was to stay overnight, a stopover between Nakhl and the next stop farther south.

In a very short time the Red Sea coast came into view—a magnificent sight that I was in no mood to appreciate (plate 46). The oil-drilling facilities and the oil workers camp could be clearly seen ahead of us. The helicopter was flying lower and lower, and we were now following a concrete paved road built by the Israelis that was now mostly covered with windblown sand. The pilot saw a clear stretch of road and brought the helicopter down there. As he touched down, he shouted: Everybody out!

Dumbfounded, I and my two companions and the unidentified man stepped out onto the road. As the rotors stopped and we could hear each other, Abbas stepped forward to me. I was looking at him with blood in mind. He pulled the unidentified man toward me. This is Mr. So-and-So (I don't recall the name he stated), the owner of the helicopter company, Abbas said; he will explain.

It was there, in the middle of nowhere, surrounded by sand dunes, beside the idling helicopter, that I learned the truth. The only way Abbas Nadim could manage to get a helicopter for me was to find an accomplice to do a little cheating. This helicopter company serviced the oil companies, flying their people from the Ras Sudr facility to two other oil facilities on the Sinai coast, and to Suez City, shuttling the workers or engineers back and forth. The owner was paid off by Abbas to arrange for a shuttling this morning by an empty helicopter, to pick up people at Ras Sudr and bring them to Suez City (at the head of the Gulf of Suez). But instead of flying the usual route, along the coastline, a detour was arranged, to accommodate my wish to visit the mountain. But because we started late, the helicopter could not linger at the mountain, because it had to be at Ras Sudr by a certain time.

I shook my head with disbelief. There was no other way to get a helicopter, Abbas told me. I knew that he was right, because I had tried and tried without success. "But why are we stopped here?" I asked. "Why doesn't the helicopter take us to the village or to the oilworkers camp?"

The owner of the company spoke up. "Because no one knows what I did," he admitted. "I am not allowed to take anyone except the oil company employees. If I take you to the camp, they will ask me: 'Who are these people?'!"

"What about taking us to the village, where we have overnight accommodations?" I suggested.

"No, the villagers will squeal on me. There's a big house just ahead," he said, pointing it out. "Go there, they will give you a ride to the village."

The helicopter's rotors started turning.

"This is unbelievable," I said disgustedly. "This is incredible! Let me at least have pictures to prove it was not a dream, a desert mirage!" The pictures were taken; here is one, showing Harvey beside the helicopter (plate 47).

The adventures that followed would take too long to describe. It was only after nightfall that we managed to rejoin the group, which had been taken by the tour bus from Nakhl to the overnight accommodations. It turned out that Abbas knew that we would never rejoin the group in Nakhl, so the plan was for his assistant, his Cairo manager, to take the group in the bus to the Ras Sudr village without waiting for the three of us to return. They too, we learned, had had their share of adventures: The bus driver, seeking a shortcut rather than following paved roads, had gotten lost . . .

It was a beautiful morning the next day. Some of the group swam in the Red Sea. We drove south, stopped at the hot springs resort used by Pharaohs, drove via Wadi Firan to the monastery of St. Catherine. We had overnight accommodations at the Peace Village that Sadat envisaged, so that once more, in a way, my path and his crossed. The hardy ones in our group climbed Mount Mussa next morning. In the afternoon we visited the monastery, and I pointed out the sign that confirms that Mount Mussa, alias Mount Sinai, was of lesser height than the St. Katherine mountain (see fig. 96, page 135).

So why did I take the group there if Mount Sinai, the real Mount Sinai, was not there? To leave no doubt in their minds, for all the reasons enumerated earlier, that this mountain could not be the Mount of the Exodus.

But did I obtain proof that my choice, near Nakhl, was the true

Mount Sinai? All I had obtained on this adventure was the two eyewitnesses, Abbas and Harvey, confirming that a round object, UFO-like, was seen atop the mountain. And I had the new photographs, this time in color. But the on-the-spot verification did not take place.

"We will have to have another tour and another helicopter," I told Abbas.

"Inshallah [God willing]," he said, smiling.

"No Inshallah," I said; *"you* owe me a helicopter!"

***

Later that year Abbas called me with good news: The Egyptian authorities, recognizing the Sinai's touristic potential, were relaxing the rules. Some tour companies were planning tours by helicopter; permits might be granted. Before long he reported that he was sure that a helicopter for a private flight could be obtained. With Israel by then also at peace with Jordan, he had a bright idea: Let's have a Peace Tour, he said—Israel, Egypt, Jordan (and the Sinai in between). I liked the idea; there are places in Jordan I really want to explore, I said, like Mount Nebo, where Moses died, and the place where Elijah was taken up to heaven. There are places like Petra and Jerash, he said. We started working on an encompassing itinerary.

Listing all the must-see places that no one going to these countries, certainly if for the first time, should miss, plus the special places I wanted to include, plus the helicopter flight, the length of the planned tour became unmanageable. Agreeing with me that Israel, with myriad archaeological and religious sites, needed a tour of its own, Abbas reduced the grand Peace Tour to Egypt, Sinai, and Jordan. As we contemplated itineraries, a key question was where the helicopter flight would originate. Abbas reported that he could obtain a helicopter for a flight based on Taba, where the Taba Hilton Hotel had a functioning helicopter pad.

Taba, a sandy beach on the coast of the Gulf of Eilat (also known as the Gulf of Aqaba) just south of Eilat proper, was where the Israelis built a resort hotel as part of the development of tourist facilities and attractions—a pier for glass-bottom boats, a sports club, an underwater observatory and aquarium, and then the Taba hotel—all built to capitalize on the magnificent Gulf views, the coral reefs, and the colorful fish of the Red Sea. After the Egyptian-Israeli Peace Treaty was signed, the Egyptians claimed that the international border ran not south of the hotel, as had been believed, but just north of it—so that the hotel belonged to Egypt. After years of discussions, negotiations, and suggested compromises, with each side producing old maps and British and Ottoman documents, an international tribunal ruled in favor of Egypt. They, in turn, gave it to the Hilton chain to manage.

On February 6, 1995, after a week of touring in Egypt proper, my group was taken to the Sinai by bus, arriving at the Taba Hilton toward the end of the day. The plan was for the helicopter to pick up Abbas and me the next morning at 6:00 A.M. and bring us back to the hotel by 8:00 A.M., in time to join the group in a leisurely breakfast and then the day's activities (a tour of the red-rock canyons, ancient copper mines, a boat ride in the Gulf, and swimming among the coral reefs). As we checked in, the hotel seemed busier than expected. My wife and I went to our room. Its windows looked out on a barbed-wire fence just a few feet away—the new international border with Israel. It was not a pleasant view.

Minutes later the phone rang. It was Abbas; he had to talk to me urgently. I met him in the lobby. He had bad news: There would be no helicopter tomorrow morning; the hotel was hosting an international meeting and the airspace was closed!

A few inquiries apprised us that the U.S. Secretary of Commerce Ronald Brown, who had been shuttling between Egypt, Israel, and Jordan as part of American efforts to enhance peace in the area through trade and economic activity, had decided to meet the trade representatives of Egypt, Israel, Jordan, and the Palestinians before he returned to the States. On short notice, a two-day meeting had been called, and Taba's Hilton Hotel had been chosen as the venue. While the Secretary was there, nongovernmental flights were prohibited for security reasons.

I then noticed that everywhere in the hotel there were young crew-cut men wearing dark blue suits and white shirts with wires coming out of their ears; it wasn't difficult to figure out who they were. I got hold of the American chief of security and explained to him who I was, the importance of my research, my contacts with the media, and all the other reasons why *my* flight tomorrow morning should be permitted. His answer was short: Do it after two days.

Reporting to Abbas, I told him that I was prepared to postpone departure for two days. Let the group go ahead with the tour as planned, I said. I would catch up with them in Amman (in Jordan). At my insistence he called the helicopter company's manager. The answer was that

that was not possible—the helicopter was booked for other flights on the other days.

My wife tried to console me. "You'll do it another time," she reassured me. I didn't think so, and until now there has been no other time.

I saw what I had seen, my photographs show what they show. Now I share them with my readers for the first time.

Is the round white feature a mechanical object, a UFO? Or is it a natural formation, carved by rain and wind? I would prefer the former, though it might well prove to be the latter.

But there is no possible natural explanation for the perfectly circular cave entrance in the oddly shaped promontory, with its series of spaced openings and manicured top. They remain a mystery atop the Elusive Mount.

12

A TOWER TO REACH HEAVEN

O f all the unique constructed places on Earth, there is only one that has existed since before the Great Flood, the biblical Deluge. Five thousand years ago a Sumerian king went to this place in search of immortality. In 1998, a group of fans went there with me to find out why the Sumerians had called the place The Landing Place, and who it was who built it with stone blocks so colossal that there are none like them elsewhere on Earth.

Nowadays the place is known as Baalbek, the place belonging to the Lord of the Valley. The ancient Greeks called it Heliopolis, City of the Sun god (Helios). The Phoenicians before them named the place in their tales of the gods "the Fastness of Zaphon," a term that meant both North and Secret, a place where the god Ba'al (simply meaning the Lord) had a secret hideaway. The Bible knew the place as Beth-Shemesh, "the Abode of Shamash," the Sun god. And the Sumerian king who had gone there before them all, Gilgamesh, simply called it The Landing Place, for that is what it was.

Gilgamesh was the fifth king in a dynasty appointed by the gods to be kings or high priests (or both) in the Sumerian city of Uruk, a royal city known as Erech in the Bible. Like the founder of the dynasty, one Meskiaggasher, Gilgamesh was a demigod. But unlike his predecessors, who were fathered by a god, it was the mother of Gilgamesh who was a goddess; her name was Ninsun. Sumerian artists depicted both Gilgamesh and his divine mother in sculptures and on cylinder seals (fig. 104).

Figure 104

Significantly, because his divine parent was a goddess (his father was the High Priest of Uruk), Gilgamesh was considered not just a demigod—he was deemed to have been two-thirds divine. As he grew older and began to contemplate the issues of life and death, he appealed to his mother and to his godfather, the god Utu/Shamash, and asked why could he not escape mortality if he was two-thirds, not just half, divine? After a lecture that the gods, when they created Man, gave Mankind Knowledge but not Immortality, a celestial object landed in Uruk. It was accepted as a heavenly omen that Gilgamesh should be given the opportunity to seek immortality. To do that, he was told, he had to enter the Landing Place and there ascend heavenward to reach the abode of the gods.

The saga of the first recorded Search For Immortality is now known as the *Epic of Gilgamesh,* originally a memoir in Sumerian by the king himself and then rendered in Akkadian and other ancient languages, and best preserved in its Akkadian (Babylonian and Assyrian) language inscribed on twelve clay tablets. It describes not one but two "in-search-of" journeys; the first one (which ended in failure) was to the Landing Place in the Cedar Mountain—the only area in the Near East whose description fits the famed forest of cedar trees in Lebanon.

The "secret place of the gods" in the Cedar Forest, Gilgamesh was told, could be entered only through a secret tunnel whose entrance was guarded by a fierce, fire-belching mechanical monster. Access was further complicated because the forest was the abode of the Bull of Heaven, the sacred animal of the god Enlil. Concerned for her son's safety, Ninsun prevailed on an android called Enkidu to accompany Gilgamesh and protect him.

The journey was not without heart-stopping incidents, omen-filled dreams, and repeated efforts by Enkidu to dissuade Gilgamesh from pushing on. But Gilgamesh insisted on proceeding. Even if I fail, he said, at least it will always be said that I tried. Finally the two arrived at the Cedar Mountain. "They looked at the height of the cedar trees, they looked for the entrance to the forest. They beheld the Cedar Mountain, abode of the gods."

Awestruck and tired, Gilgamesh and Enkidu lay down to rest and sleep, planning to find the entrance in the morning. During the night Gilgamesh had several dreams, and he was awakened by someone passing by; he was unsure whether it was a god. Then he was awakened by an "overpowering glare." What he saw was "wholly awesome":

> The heavens shrieked, the earth boomed.
> Though daylight was dawning, darkness came.
> Lightning flashed, a flame shot up.
> The clouds swelled, it rained death!
> Then the glow vanished, the fire went out,
> And all that had fallen was turned to ashes.

With these words from the millennia-old epic, what Gilgamesh is stated to have witnessed was a sight that I, and all of you, have seen more than once on our television screens: *the launching of a rocketship or shuttlecraft by NASA* (plate 48). And the awesome sight confirmed to Gilgamesh that he had indeed arrived at the Landing Place, the place where he could join the gods in a journey to their celestial abode.

How and why the two failed to attain their purpose is described in the rest of the epic (and in my book *The Stairway to Heaven*). What is important is that, reading those lines, I was convinced that Gilgamesh had actually witnessed the nighttime launching of a rocketship. A depiction on a Phoenician coin, showing the temple of Ba'al with a rocketlike object in its protected area (fig. 105), convinced me that Baalbek in Lebanon was one and the same as the Landing Place that was the destination of Gilgamesh.

Figure 105

And so it was that the "Plus" in the 1998 Earth Chronicles Expedition "Syria Plus" (fig. 106) was not at all in Syria, but in Lebanon. Going there entailed complex border crossings; coordination of tour buses and guides from two jurisdictions (the Syrian bus and guide could

IS PROUD TO ANNOUNCE THE ULTIMATE EXPEDITION
WITH

ZECHARIA SITCHIN

SYRIA PLUS...
AUGUST 28—SEPTEMBER 10, 1998

* Journey to a time before the flood and experience the legacies of gods, legendary kings and heroes with the internationally acclaimed author of <u>The Stairway to Heaven</u> and <u>Divine Encounters.</u>
* Follow in the footsteps of Gilgamesh, King of Sumer 5,000 years ago, to the **LANDING PLACE**
* Visit Mari, on the Euphrates River, where the goddess Ishtar crowned "The Psalmist of the gods" to be King 4,000 years ago.
* Roam the legendary kingdom-states of Ugarit and Ebla, sites of discovery of priceless clay tablets.
*Climb the ramparts of the Crusaders largest castle ever built.
* Stay at Palmyra, a pearl of Graeco-Roman temples, a desert Oasis that the Bible called Tadmor and King Solomon built.
* Immerse yourself in the fabled cities of Damascus, Homs, Dier Ezzor, Aleppo, and their citadels, Mosques, bazaars, Museums filled with hidden treasures.
* Enjoy the privilege of on-site and special briefing by Zecharia Sitchin.

Figure 106

not enter Lebanon, and vice versa); complex bureaucratic paperwork, visas, and permits; inspection stops en route and at the border by men, both uniformed and in mufti, emitting suspicious stares. The trip also carried no small measure of risk, for the area of Baalbek had been taken over as a center and training ground for some of the most vicious Middle Eastern terrorist groups, whose claim to fame came from suicide bombings and the abduction and execution of Israelis and Westerners (Americans in particular). But sensing that political-military circumstances opened a window of opportunity of relative safety, an Expedition that I had envisioned and planned for quite some time was launched on short notice. Only selected veterans of previous Expeditions were invited to come. And thus, on a memorable day—September 1, 1998—we crossed the border from Syria to Lebanon and returned after spending a full day at the most unique place on Earth. The planning, the apprehension, the risk, were all worthwhile.

✳✳✳

We left our hotel, the Damascus Sheraton, in the wee hours of the morning in order to reach the Lebanese border at "opening time," but when we got there our tour bus had to join a long line of trucks and cars that were already waiting. The crossing procedures were lengthy and complex, as we (a tour group of Americans) were a rarity and engendered no small amount of suspicion on the one hand and a desire to show hospitality on the other hand. But finally, in a new bus and with a new guide, we were off on our way in Lebanon.

A drive, much longer than we anticipated, finally brought us to an intersection where a sign with an arrow announced "To the Roman ruins." The town of Baalbek's houses, densely built, encroached on the ruins and obscured them, but as we neared our destination, the ruins' signature profile, known to us from photographs and drawings (fig. 107) came into view: the six imposing, still standing columns of the Temple of Jupiter. The bus came to a stop in a small plaza, and then it was a short walk to a most intriguing and puzzling place.

It was European travelers to the Levant (the countries of the eastern Mediterranean) who began to report in the past couple of centuries about the ruins, calling them Roman Ruins. What is visible from a distance and what seems to attract the attention of most visitors are indeed the remains of temples built by the Romans to honor and worship four of their

Figure 107

deities. The grandest of them was dedicated to Jupiter (called Zeus by the Greeks). In size it dwarfs the Parthenon in Athens. In the height of its columns—six of which remain standing—it surpasses the immense columns of the Temple of Amun in Karnak, Egypt. Moreover, it surpassed in size and grandeur the temples to Jupiter built in Rome itself, or anywhere else in the Roman Empire. Beside it the Romans erected three more temples, smaller but no less imposing—to Venus, Mercury, and (perhaps) to Bacchus (fig. 108—a nineteenth-century rendering by German researchers).

Roman construction of these temples began in the first century B.C., when Rome began to take over the lands on the eastern Mediterranean coast. The construction work to build the temples, courtyards, steps, altars, shrines, and other monumental and elaborate features of the sacred compound continued into the third century A.D. Many Roman caesars toiled to glorify this remote and strange place. Emperors and generals came to it in search of oracles; Roman legionnaires sought to be billeted near it.

But why did the Romans build their greatest temple to Jupiter not in

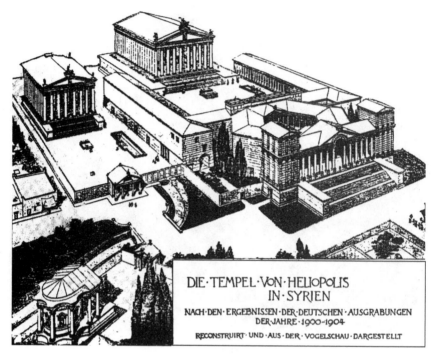

DIE·TEMPEL·VON·HELIOPOLIS
IN·SYRIEN
NACH·DEN·ERGEBNISSEN·DER·DEUTSCHEN·AUSGRABUNGEN
DER·JAHRE·1900–1904
RECONSTRUIRT·UND·AUS·DER·VOGELSCHAU·DARGESTELLT

Figure 108

Rome but here? What prompted them, over four centuries, to invest and spend wealth and labor here, and why was the place deemed sacred and hallowed?

The only explanation available is that the Romans venerated the place because the Greeks did so before them, having considered the site a twin or namesake of the Heliopolis in Egypt—the city that the Egyptians called Annu (On in the Bible). Accordingly, it is explained, the Roman name for Jupiter when worshipped here was Jupiter Heliopolitanus; and statues, altars, and even coins honoring him bore the tetragrammaton IOHM—Iovi Optimo Maximo Heliopolitano, "Jove of Heliopolis, the optimal and maximal god."

The Greek counterparts of the deities that the Romans venerated at this Heliopolis (some say it was Alexander the Great who suggested the naming) were Zeus, Aphrodite, and Hermes, and, of course, also Helios, the Sun god. Whatever Greek temples may have actually stood there is not certain, because the Romans cleared away earlier temples to make room for their own. Those who followed the Romans—Byzantines, Moslems, Crusaders—also did their best to substitute their churches or mosques for the previous temples, doing their best to obliterate previous religious edifices.

But nothing that was done atop the vast stone platform on which all those temples stood could destroy the platform itself, with the maze of substructures under it and the massive stone blocks that supported it. Most enduring has been the northwestern corner where the retaining walls, as can be seen from the outside, include stone blocks of incredible size, precisely cut and placed, including the three colossal stone blocks that are the largest in the world, the famed *Trilithon* (see nineteenth-century illustration, fig. 109).

The designation of the site as Roman ruins stems from the fact that it is largely what the Romans built that remains standing atop the platform, while subsequent Christian or Moslem ones have fallen apart, victim both to time and climate ravages, as well as to not infrequent earthquakes in the area. But all these structures, of whatever era and faith, were

Figure 109

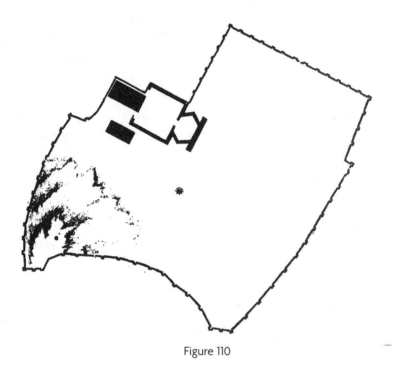

Figure 110

erected upon the original platform of stone pavings. We know from descriptions by travelers in the seventeenth, eighteenth, and nineteenth centuries and the reports of archaeologists in the twentieth century (mostly German before World War I, mostly French thereafter) how extensive the original sacred area was (fig. 110). With some sides measuring 2,500 feet, it encompassed an area of five million square feet. How much of it was paved with stones to create a platform cannot be determined nowadays because houses, constantly built closer and closer to the sacred site, now encroach upon it almost to the unique northwestern corner, where the remaining ruins are. It is there that the most massive retaining walls can be seen (fig. 111).

Baalbek is situated on the western slope of the Anti-Lebanon range, which is separated from the Lebanon range on the west by the Bekka—"cleft" or "valley" (hence the name Ba'al-Bek, the place of the Lord of the Cleft/Valley). This valley or cleft runs in a northeast–southwest direction. The special corner deliberately formed thus afforded to its creators an unimpeded approach and view on three sides, even on the mountainside facing the valley and the next mountain range. It was at that unimpeded corner that the various temples were built atop the earlier base (fig. 112).

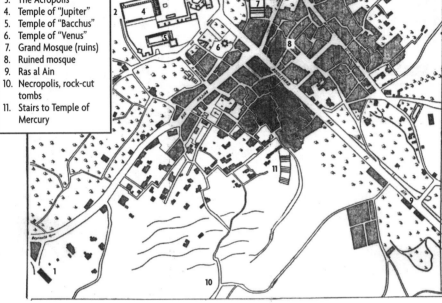

Baalbek

1. Largest cut stone in the world
2. Trilithon
3. The Acropolis
4. Temple of "Jupiter"
5. Temple of "Bacchus"
6. Temple of "Venus"
7. Grand Mosque (ruins)
8. Ruined mosque
9. Ras al Ain
10. Necropolis, rock-cut tombs
11. Stairs to Temple of Mercury

Figure 111

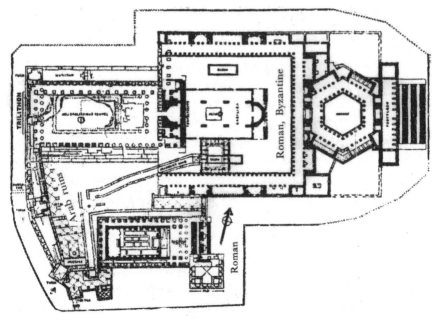

Figure 112

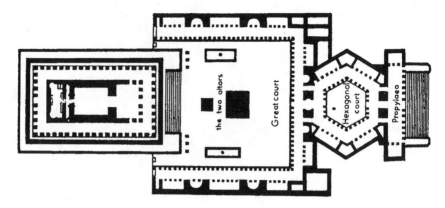

Figure 113

The Jupiter temple proper occupies the western end of a series of imposing structures. They begin at the eastern end of the temple complex with a monumental stairway that led to an entrance section, rectangular in shape, called Propylaion; it was marked by two towers connected by a colonnade. This led to a hexagonal court surrounded by minor structures, and through it to a great square court with altars, columns, side shrines, and other functional structures. All that finally led to the grand temple of Jupiter itself—more than 1,000 feet in all (fig. 113). The current remains or ruins in the courtyard section are those of the Basilica of Theodosius, built by the Byzantines when they converted the courtyard to a church.

No sooner does a visitor pass through the main entrance gate in the southeast than looming in front of him (or her) is literally a stone mountain that rises and rises in a series of steps and platforms. As the visitor tackles the first series of steps up to the Jupiter temple, another level comes into view. The temple, one realizes, stood not upon the original platform but on a smaller raised level at the northwestern corner. It was called the Podium and it rose sixteen feet above its foundation level; as a view from the south makes clear (plate 49 and fig. 114), it also stood upon rows of perfectly shaped and medium-sized cut stone blocks weighing several tons each. Those, in turn, were placed upon a base of immense stone blocks, also perfectly shaped and cut, estimated to weigh more than 500 tons each. And all of this stood upon another lower-level platform that itself was raised high above the general, larger basic platform.

Having done the climbing all this way up, and after a rest stop in the

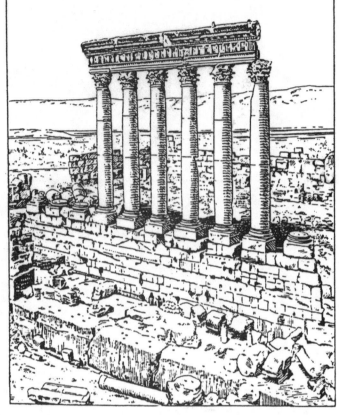

Figure 114

shade available beside the six standing columns, we had had enough of the local guide's narrative and it was time to start our own investigation. It led, first and foremost, out through the Jupiter temple all the way back and around the ruins, to the western retaining wall with its immense stone blocks, including the famed Trilithon (plate 50 and fig. 115). The stone blocks that make up the Trilithon weigh more than 1,100 tons each, and they do not lie on the ground itself, but are placed higher, upon other immense, though smaller, stone blocks, cut to have a slanting face, that weigh "only" 500 tons each. (By comparison, the stone blocks in the Giza pyramid average only 2.5 tons.)

There is even now no man-made machine that can lift such weights. Yet in antiquity someone—the "giants," according to local lore—not only lifted and placed such colossal stone blocks, but also carried them from their quarry located several miles away. This is an indisputable fact,

Figure 115

because the quarry has been located and in it one of those colossal stone blocks, whose quarrying had not been completed, still lies partly attached to the native rock. Its immensity is illustrated by the many photographs we took there; its size exceeds that of the Trilithon blocks (plates 51 and 52).

As we spent hours investigating the ruins, we found that the Trilithon and the other colossal stone blocks in the western wall were matched by other stone blocks, especially where the retaining walls formed corners; there, the corner stones were not two stones meeting at an angle, but were formed of a single immense stone block cut and shaped to provide a ninety-degree corner. Everywhere the original stone blocks were immense; where later additions were made, the stone blocks are much smaller and look pitiful by comparison.

Whatever once stood upon the immense platform, other than in its cut-out northwestern part, one can only speculate. It is clear, however, that whoever planned, constructed, quarried, and transported the colossal stone blocks and then placed them one on top of another had a specific purpose in mind. Whatever went on there in the ancient past seems to have required this massive structure that rose up and up by massive stages.

To our astonishment we discovered, as we climbed upon this northwestern corner over and over again, that at some places the Trilithon blocks were exposed on top, with nothing laid above them. On those exposed faces we could see grooves, cut into the stones diagonally. With compasses we checked orientations, but there did not seem to be any astronomical (solstice, equinox) associations. The grooves must have had architectural or structural purpose; what it was we could not tell.

I had with me sketches made by German researchers who took a special interest in the place in preparation for a visit by the Kaiser before World War I. They showed the massiveness of the podium on which the Jupiter temple stood as seen from outside and how much it rose above ground level (fig. 116). But sketches of the crosscuts revealed that the

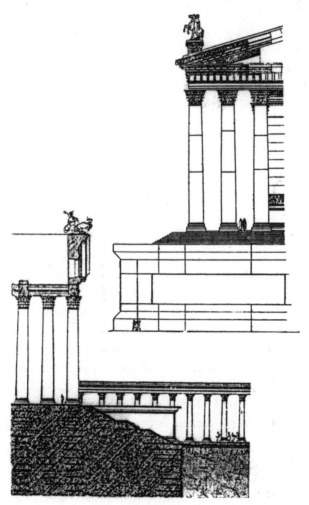

Figure 116

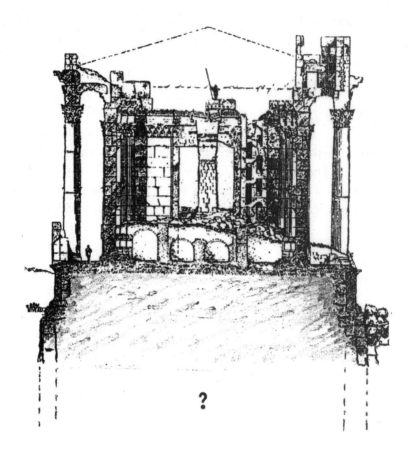

Figure 117

area on which the temple rose was in fact a landfill, with subsurface passageways, archways, and other cavities. This landfill in turn rested upon a stone floor at some deeper, undetermined level (fig. 117). The German engineers did not (or could not) determine how far down this landfilled hollow went. It seems that it went all the way down to the base of the retaining walls; but did these walls, as now exposed, continue with more courses (rows) to bedrock? How much further down was the bedrock, and did the hollow continue into bedrock? We had no way of telling.

We left at the end of the day exhilarated, satisfied that we could corroborate many answers to the enigmas posed by the place, but at the same time besieged with an array of new questions. Both aspects of the visit were discussed not only on the return drive but also at the hotel until late at night; no one felt like going to sleep after having been to the place where Gilgamesh had gone, where the Anunnaki had been, a place that was built before the Flood. In these conversations the most oft repeated words were "massive," "colossal," "giant," and the like, for it was the incomprehensible massiveness of the place that astounded most—gigantic stones placed one atop the other, held together without mortar, rising stage after stage to incredible heights, and all placed on a vast stone platform.

In *The Stairway to Heaven* I have shown that Baalbek was incorporated into the post-Diluvial Landing Corridor of the Anunnaki at the very beginning of the planning of a spaceport in the Sinai (to replace the one in Mesopotamia that was wiped out by the Deluge). This was done by running a line from the peaks of Ararat through Baalbek and extending it to Giza, where the pyramids were to be built (see fig. 97, page 138). A key confirmation of this conclusion was the fact that the Bekka valley-cleft indeed ran in conformity with such a line, from northeast to southwest. Both the Great Pyramid (GZ in fig. 97) and the other anchor (in the Sinai peninsula, US in fig. 97) that in the end delineated the Landing Corridor were equidistant from Baalbek, confirming that it had already existed when the planning was made, and since the new spaceport was needed only after the Deluge, Baalbek had to exist from before the Deluge.

Baalbek is located where, according to all modern and recent studies, the "domestication" of cereals and other food crops began. According to Sumerian tales of Enlil and Enki, it was they who engaged in genetic engineering to do just that on the "Holy Mount," a place readily available after the Deluge. We were convinced that it was upon the vast stone platform, surviving the Deluge, that all that had occurred. We were satisfied that the location in the Cedar Forest—there is no other cedar forest anywhere else—and the various tunnels and other subsurface features of Baalbek fit the descriptions in the *Epic of Gilgamesh,* and thus confirm it as his "Landing Place."

But we found the depiction on the Phoenician coin confusing, for it showed the rocketlike object poised on a platform, and fenced *only on three sides.* So what was the purpose of the massive retaining walls, and why did they rise up and up and up?

Another key new puzzle was the realization that the main part of the Jupiter temple, located at the westernmost end of the series of steps, courts, etc., stood not on original ground, but on an artificial podium that was placed on top of lower stages; and the area of the podium was actually a landfill—it covered a hollow that went down to undetermined depth. What was that for?

We had to admit that the northwestern corner and its colossal stone blocks and overwhelming massiveness remained a puzzle.

***

It was only a year later, back in the United States, that I found the solution to the problem that kept bothering me: If the massiveness of the construction indicated that launchings took place at the northwestern corner, why was there a deep cavity surrounded by massive walls?

I was giving a lecture at Cocoa Beach in Florida and took the opportunity to visit the nearby NASA facility at Cape Canaveral, from which the shuttles and other spacecraft are launched. The official tour included some of the huge hangars where the spacecraft and their propelling rockets are housed, the giant moving platform that transports those monsters to the launch pads, and some of the launch pads themselves. The latter, it turned out, are not "pads" at all, but actually towering steel structures, multileveled, into the midst of which the rockets are wheeled; then they "embrace" or enclose the rocket and its payload. The various levels of this steel tower provide access to various parts of the vehicle to be launched, allowing technicians to service the vehicle, fuel it, and escort the astronauts to their module or shuttle.

And it was only on seeing that that I realized what I had seen in Baalbek: It was a *launch tower,* built not of steel but of massive stones!

The massive stones, I realized, formed an enclosure that surrounded a cavity, an empty space or hollow within which stood the rocket about to be launched. The encompassing walls were multileveled, rising in stages, just as modern steel launch towers have to be to enable servicing the rocketship and its payload, such as a command module. At Baalbek, the arriving rocketships in all probability landed on the vast stone platform adjoining the launch tower; then they would be lifted, carried, and put in place—as had been done to the colossal quarried stone blocks!—within the massive stone enclosure, ready for launching. It was from that spot, the northwestern corner, that the rocketship whose launching Gilgamesh witnessed had risen skyward.

And I and my group had stood upon and *inside* that launch tower! (plate 53)

And when Mankind tried to emulate this by building a launch tower made of bricks, in the place the Bible called Babel, they were only emulating the real one that the gods themselves had built in the Cedar Mountain:

> And the Lord came down
> to see the city and the tower
> that the children of the Adam were building.
> And the Lord said:
> Behold, they are one people and have one language,
> and this is what they had begun to do;
> and now they could achieve all that they had planned.
> Let us come down, and confound their language
> that they may not understand each other's speech.
> And the Lord scattered them from there
> upon the face of the Earth,
> and they ceased to build the city.
> —Genesis 11:4–8

But at Baalbek one can still climb the remains of the original "Tower of Babel"—the one built by the gods themselves to reach heaven.

***

Postscript

In October 2003, China launched an astronaut into space, thereby laying a claim to membership in the exclusive club of nations (the United States and Russia) with such a capability. The secrecy surrounding the feat was only partly lifted by the release of some bare-bones information and photographs by the Chinese government, but even such scant information was most enlightening to me.

First there was the name chosen for the command module, the capsule holding the astronaut atop the rocket. It was named *Shenzou* and the official releases explained that in Chinese it meant "divine vessel"—a name that evoked the very terms used in antiquity for the flying vehicles of the gods.

That alone was reason for me to say, Wow!

Figure 118

Then there was the shape of the command module, the actual "divine boat" employed by the Chinese. The shape, shown in the released materials (fig. 118), was uncannily similar to the shape of the "command module" in which the angel of the Lord appeared to Abraham on Mount Moriah! (See fig. 79 on page 103 in the chapter about the UFO in the buried synagogue.)

And, last but not least, the Chinese launch tower drew my interest. As the released photographs showed (fig. 119), the steel structure embraced the rocketship on *three sides* only; the fourth side was open to the immense paved platform stretching in the direction from where the spacecraft was moved (wheeled?) *into* the rising launch tower.

Figure 119

And, all at once, I realized why the *stone* launch tower at Baalbeck rose only on three sides, with the fourth facing a vast open stone platform. It was through that open fourth side that the rocketships were brought into the tower.

13

TUNNELS FOR TIME TRAVEL

This chapter is a tale of two tunnels. They are both in Jerusalem, in Israel. They are both nothing short of being Time Machines. One takes the visitor to the days of Judean kings, a few thousand years ago. The other, which is not really a tunnel, takes the visitor to the legendary past, when gods, not men, reigned there, and it may even portend the future.

Similar and different, both can best be understood if one travels to other lands. Luckily, I, and then the Expeditions groups joining me, have gone to those places.

First, the real tunnel—because it is easier to explain and because it is one of the clearest instances of physical evidence that corroborates the Bible. It is the tunnel best known as Hezekiah's Tunnel. It connects, below ground, the Spring of Gihon on the outskirts of Jerusalem with the Silo'am Pool inside the walls of ancient Jerusalem (fig. 120). Its existence was at first known only from the Bible, which means that it could be either deemed unquestionable holy writ or doubted as the fancy of scribes; but now one can see it all in person.

A visit to the tunnel takes the visitor first to a time of great turmoil in the Near East; though these words well apply to the present, we are talking about the seventh and sixth centuries B.C., when mighty Assyria was the dominant power. Its domains encompassed peoples and lands far flung in all directions, even as far as Egypt in Africa; but on the way there, the empire's armies had to cross the narrow geographic bridge where the

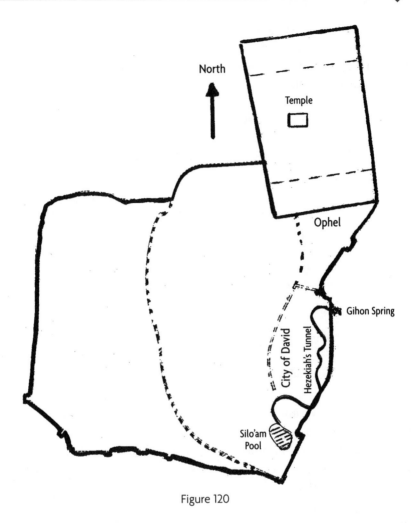

Figure 120

successors of David and Solomon were kings. By the time of Hezekiah (727–686 B.C.), only the southern part of the Hebrew kingdom, Judea, with its capital Jerusalem, remained independent; the northern part, known as the kingdom of Israel, was already overrun by the Assyrians, and its people (later known as the Ten Lost Tribes) were in exile.

Having been attacked before, and anticipating a new attack and siege by the army of the Assyrian king Sennacherib, King Hezekiah reinforced the fortifications of Jerusalem and embarked on an ingenious project to ensure the city's water supply. Under his orders, an underground tunnel was secretly cut through the rocks to connect a pool, the Pool of Silo'am inside the city walls, with a major water source, the Spring of Gihon, which was located well outside the city walls. An invader, it was hoped, would not realize that the city continued to draw water from the distant spring. The Bible mentioned Hezekiah's feat in II Kings 20:21 and II Chronicles 32:30:

> And the rest of the acts of Hezekiah
> and all his might,
> And how he made a pool and a conduit
> and brought water into the city—
> Are they not written in the
> book of the chronicles of Judah?
>
> This same Hezekiah also blocked the
> upper watercourse of Gihon,
> And brought it directly down to the
> west side of the City of David.

In the nineteenth century, astounding discoveries were being made, mostly by archaeologists excavating under the auspices of the British Museum, in the Tigris region in northern Mesopotamia. Cities known hitherto only from the Bible, such as the Assyrian capital, were found and unearthed. Palaces and temples saw the light of day again. Discovered were also libraries with tens of thousands of cuneiform tablets. Many formed parts of royal libraries and archives, containing the annals of the kings of Assyria. In one of those royal records, known as the Taylor Prism, which is on display in the British Museum in London (fig. 121), the Assyrian king Sennacherib described the siege of Jerusalem when Hezekiah the Judean reigned there!

The Bible (II Kings chapter 19) relates that the siege by the army of Sennacherib failed because one night the Angel of the Lord smote the Assyrian camp. The annals of Sennacherib skip over how or why the siege of Jerusalem ended abruptly; but otherwise the cuneiform inscriptions found in Nineveh corroborate the biblical record of Hezekiah and the siege of Jerusalem.

But does that mean that the story of the tunnel was also corroborated?

That such a tunnel could be cut through the hard rocks of Jerusalem's hills over a substantial length (almost 2,000 feet) led not a few scholars to doubt the veracity of the biblical record, although the existence (to this day) of the Gihon Spring and the existence (to this very day) of the

Figure 121

Silo'am Pool are undisputed. At the beginning of the nineteenth century, shepherd boys found the entrance to a tunnel at the spring, and in 1838 the explorer Edward Robinson found and traversed its full length. In subsequent decades other explorers cleared and examined the tunnel and its various shafts and branches, establishing that it indeed connected and enabled water to flow from the spring to the pool inside the city as it had in Hezekiah's time.

But does that also mean that it was an artificial tunnel, cut by Hezekiah?

It was in 1880 that an incredible discovery was made: an inscription left behind by the tunnel's ancient builders (or cutters). About midway in the tunnel they smoothed a section of the wall and placed an inscription that commemorated a major event—the meeting at that spot of the rock cutters, who were tunneling from both ends!

The inscription, in beautiful Hebrew script of the time (fig. 122), stated the following in the undamaged portions:

> . . . the tunnel. And this is the account of the breakthrough. When [the tunnelers lifted] the axe each toward his fellow, and while there were still three cubits to be tunneled [through], the voice of a man was heard calling to his fellow, for there was a crack in the rock on the right . . . And on the day of the breakthrough the tunnelers struck each toward his comrade, axe to axe. And the water started to flow from its source to the pool, a thousand and two hundred cubits. And the height of the rock above the heads of the tunnelers was one hundred cubits.

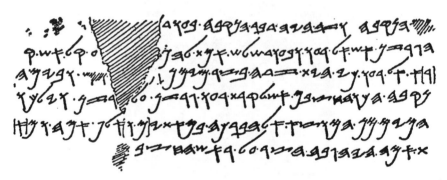

Figure 122

Nowadays the spring lies downhill from Jerusalem's Old City, at the village of Silwan. The Israeli authorities built a modern and comfortable entranceway to Hezekiah's Water Tunnel (fig. 123). Some might be satisfied with viewing the small, museum-like exhibit, then going down spiraling stairs to the cavernlike beginning of the tunnel (fig. 124; plate 54).

Others (who included most of my group) donned knee-high waterproof boots (provided by the tunnel guides) and went through the

Figure 123

Figure 124

whole length of the tunnel, to emerge within the ancient city's walls. Though the underground trek, lasting about forty minutes, is made easy by the installation of stairs, handrails, and lighting, the eerie feeling is overpowering as one realizes that this is a walk through history, in the most literal sense. As if whisked by a time machine, one is literally in Jerusalem of Judean kings 3,000 years ago. This is no hologram, not a reconstruction to scale; this is the real thing, its depth and its length exactly as detailed in the Bible.

The engineering feat is no less awe-inspiring. The tunnel, horizontally, runs level with just a slight incline that enabled the waters to flow, but its course twists and turns, depending on the rock formation. To this day, no one has figured out how the tunnelers, who worked from both ends, managed to meet deep below ground.

Most walkers fell silent, filled with emotions and thoughts. But the silence was broken when the expected inscription failed to show up. *Where is the inscription?* the guide was repeatedly asked, as the midway point was reached and passed.

"It used to be here," the guide says as he points; but then he explains that it is no longer here. When the inscription was discovered, Jerusalem was under Ottoman rule, and the Turkish authorities chiseled out the portion of the rock on which the writing was carved and took the extracted slab to Istanbul.

That was the only disappointing part of an otherwise memorable experience—but one that was remedied on one of my tours to Turkey with an Expedition group, when I made it a point to see the actual inscription. The archaeological museum complex in Istanbul consists of several parts: the Topkapi palace, the old Museum of the Ancient Orient, and the modernized Archaeological Museum. The Museum of the Ancient Orient, which contains the earliest discoveries, including the inscribed clay tablets whose decipherment launched the career of the great Sumerologist Samuel N. Kramer, has been closed on and off for lack of funds (but was opened for me and my group by special arrangement). The Hezekiah Inscription, I learned, was displayed in the modern Archaeological Museum, and we expected to see it without problem since that museum was open during usual hours. But as we climbed up to the top floor to see the artifact, we found our way blocked by barriers. The two top floors, the guards said, were out of bounds, with all lights shut off.

I had to go back to the administrative offices to persuade them to have the darkened floors lit up and opened. Finally, we stood by the display case holding the incredible piece of rock from ancient Jerusalem (plate 55). To make what we were looking at more meaningful, I distributed to the group a sheet of paper on which the ancient Hebrew alphabet and its modern counterparts were drawn, and guided the group in reading Hezekiah's inscription and its translation.

We spent a good part of an hour there, the envy no doubt of every Bible lover: There it was, irrefutable corroboration of statements in two books (II Kings and II Chronicles) of the Old Testament.

It was ironic, though, that to refute the refuters of the Bible, in this case alone, archaeologists had to excavate in Mesopotamia, explorers and geologists had to search in Israel, and expeditions like mine had to go to museums in Britain and Turkey and travel to Israel to see the evidence come together.

***

The tunnel that connects Gihon and Silo'am holds clues to other biblical tales and to an understanding of Jerusalem's past. To reach the entrance to Hezekiah's Tunnel, which is located in the Kidron Valley to Jerusalem's east, one can take a car or a taxi or use the tour bus, or one can walk down from the southeastern edge of Jerusalem's walled Old City. I, of course, chose for my group the difficult walk on foot—difficult but not hazardous, since the Israeli authorities have built stepped paths all the way down.

To appreciate the significance of such a walk, it is best to look at a panoramic view of the area (plate 56). It shows, at the very top section, the southern part of the wall that surrounds Jerusalem's Old City (point A). This makes clear what everyone in the walk down to the Gihon Spring realized—that our destination was completely outside Jerusalem's Old City and its walls. It was a passing yet profound shock to find that before the Old City there was an older city south of it. . . . Indeed, the farther south-southeast one walks, the older the excavated remains become.

Below point A, where our tour or walkdown began, one passes by the remains of a wall (point B) believed to be part of the fortifications of Jerusalem by the exiles who had returned from Babylon in the sixth century B.C. That wall incorporates an unusual stepped structure, about

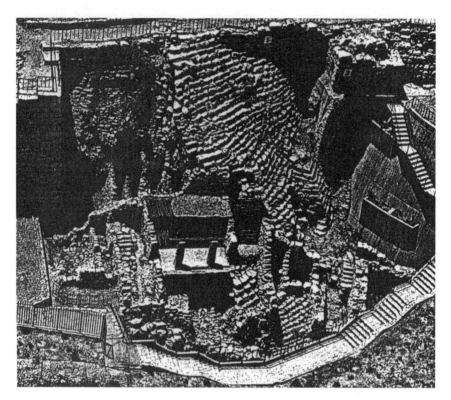

Figure 125

five stories high (point C, enlarged in fig. 125), that when excavated in 1980 caused some sensation; some referred to it as the discovery of a pyramid or ziggurat in Israel (which it is not). While the upper part of this stepped structure has been dated to a period just preceding the destruction of Jerusalem by Nebuchadnezzar of Babylon in 586 B.C., the lower portion with its arched entranceways has been dated to the Canaanite period in the thirteenth century B.C. Such datings, if accurate, do not lend support to another sensational suggestion made at the time of discovery—that these were remains of the palace of King David. But be that as it may, the structure is unusual and puzzling, and the mystery remains unresolved to this day.

Continuing down, the stairs lead the visitor past recent terracing (point D) just above the remains (point E) of an early Israelite wall dated to the tenth century B.C.—the period, in this case, of David and Solomon. The stairs then lead all the way down, to the bottom of the

Kidron Valley (point F) and the building that houses the entrance to the Tunnel.

Once beyond the walls of the Old City, the walk took place over the ruins of what is called by archaeologists the City of David. As the map (fig. 120, page 183) clarifies, it occupied a mountain spur that rises between deep valleys on all sides. According to the Bible, it was a fortified Canaanite town, inhabited by the Jebusites, going back (as the remains of the wall's bottom part in point C indicate) to the thirteenth century B.C. When David succeeded Saul as the Israelite king, his capital was Hebron, south of Jerusalem. In the eighth year of his reign, seeking a more secure location as the wars with the neighboring Philistines intensified, David set his sights on Jerusalem; but the Jebusites who resided there turned him away, secure behind their protective wall.

The capture of the Jebusite stronghold—the Bible (II Samuel 5:7) called it the Fortress of Zion—is another often questioned biblical tale proven right by modern archaeology. We are told that unable to breach the fortifications, David announced that whoever succeeded in capturing the Canaanite fortress would become commander of the king's army. His captain, Joab, accomplished the feat by using the *tzinor*—a Hebrew word rare in the Bible, but used nowadays to connote pipe or conduit.

What was the *tzinor* that enabled Joab to capture the Canaanite fortress remained a biblical puzzle until the discovery of Warren's Shaft in 1867, so named after Charles Warren, a British engineer and explorer working for the Palestine Exploration Fund of London. Examining Hezekiah's Tunnel, he discovered a vertical shaft, more than fifty feet long, that led from the water level of the Gihon Spring to an outlet at ground level within the confines of the early Canaanite city. It was presumed that the shaft was a Canaanite device for bringing up water without having to go outside the city's walls. It was also suggested in time that this was the *tzinor*—shaft, conduit—through which Joab climbed up with his men to capture the fortified city—a kind of Trojan Horse feat without a horse.

Explorations within the rocks covering the spring and its environs have revealed by now that there are other shafts and fissures, as well as remains of tunnelings prior to Hezekiah's time—some going back, perhaps, to the sixteenth century B.C. (fig. 126). Whether it was Warren's Shaft or another one of the natural or man-made conduits that let Joab in, no one can say for sure. But that this was the way into the fortress virtually everyone now agrees. These aspects of the tunnel thus demonstrate

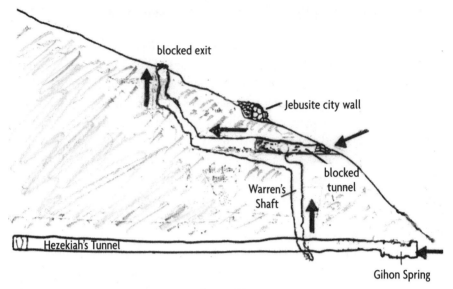

Figure 126

the feasibility of the Bible's tale of the capture of Jerusalem by David. They also establish the precise location of the "City of David."

That evening, back at the hotel, I devoted the briefing session's first part to Hezekiah's Tunnel and its implications: not so much to the events surrounding its construction, but to the implications of the evidence it offers for the location of the City of David. We have all walked downhill, I said, from where the wall surrounding the Old City is, to where the Spring of Gihon is. We have learned that David sought a better site than Hebron for his capital, one perhaps better defensible than Hebron was. So why struggle to capture the Canaanite citadel when just a few hundred feet to its north there was a *higher* location, overlooking the Canaanite city? Why, indeed, did the Canaanites, to begin with, not choose the higher site?

These were, to tell the truth, just rhetorical questions, for after hearing some opinions from the group, I proceeded to give them a Bible lesson.

To understand the matter of the site, I said, one has to recognize the role played by the Ark of the Covenant in Israelite history and its centrality to the religious and national aspects of the descendants of the Twelve Tribes that came out of Egypt to the Promised Land. Though almost four centuries have passed since their entry and settlement in Canaan (on both sides of the Jordan River), there were still skirmishes with grudging neighbors, worshippers of other gods, to the north (Arameans in Damascus), east (Ammonites), and south (Edomites). But worst was a constant and formidable adversary lodged in the southern part of the coastal plain—the Philistines (the "Sea Peoples" of Egyptian war records). Indeed, David made his first appearance on the pages of history when, as a youth, he stepped forward to challenge and slay the Philistine giantlike leader, Goliath.

Throughout their wanderings in the Sinai, the Israelites carried along with them the Ark of the Covenant, a chest covered with a layer of gold inside and out and topped by two golden cherubim (fig. 127 illustrates how it may have looked). While enshrined in the movable Tent of Appointment in the desert, it served as a *Dvir* (literally: Speaker) by which God spoke to Moses. When it came time to cross the Jordan River into Canaan proper, priests carrying the Ark by the specially designed staves waded into the river and the Ark made the waters part, so that the Israelites could cross over safely (Joshua, chapters 3 and 4). Then, during

Figure 127

crucial battles—in time mostly with the Philistines—the Ark would be brought out to the battlefield, to work its miraculous powers against the Israelites' enemies. By then the Ark was carried not by polebearers but was transported on a cart, as depicted on a stone frieze at the synagogue in Capernaum, where Jesus had worshipped according to Christian tradition (fig. 128). That apparently made it possible for the Philistines to capture it in one of the battles. Both the Philistines and the dwellers of the place where the Ark was seized were smitten for that by God, and they chose to return the Ark to the Israelites; but when an Israelite, trying to steady the Ark on the cart touched it, he too fell dead.

The Ark of the Covenant, I told my group, featured in the biblical events not only prior to the capture of the Canaanite stronghold by David, but also in the events that followed. Having ascended the throne in conflict with King Saul and his son, alienating the northern tribes, David sought to establish a new national capital (Hebron was a tribal one) both as a royal and a religious center. One of his first acts was to move the Ark of the Covenant, which was still lacking permanent housing, to a proper House of God. He intended to build such a House—a

Figure 128

temple—next to his royal palace in the City of David, and the Ark of the Covenant was indeed brought over to the City of David in a joyous ceremony. But the plans were stopped cold when the Prophet Nathan relayed to David a divine message: First, because he had shed so much blood in all the wars, it would be his son and not he who would build the House of the Lord. And secondly, that the House, the Temple of Yahweh, was to be located elsewhere—upon Mount Moriah, the very mount to the immediate north of the City of David.

What was there that prevented the Canaanites from establishing their stronghold there? What was there that made it the chosen location for the future Temple? What was there, according to those royal Davidic records, was the threshing floor of Arawna the Jebusite. That is where his oxen separated the wheat from the chaff.

To make sure that David understood the choice, and to put an end to his tarrying, an Angel of Yahweh appeared one day "upon the threshing floor of Arawna the Jebusite." He was hovering between Heaven and Earth, his drawn sword pointed at Jerusalem; and the Angel told the Prophet Gad to tell David that it was there, upon the threshing floor, that an altar to Yahweh should be erected. And David realized that "this is the place of the House of Yahweh, the place of the Altar of Sacrifice for Israel."

He was referring, I explained, to the place where Abraham had built the altar on which to sacrifice Isaac, on Mount Moriah.

So David went up as the Lord had commanded (as the Book of Samuel relates), the Hebrew noblemen with him, and told Arawna that he wished to purchase the site from him. The Jebusite, hearing what the purpose was, offered to give over the place as a gift, but David insisted on buying and paying for it. According to the Book of Samuel, he paid fifty *shekels* ("weights") of silver; according to Chronicles, the price paid was "six hundred *shekels* of gold"—quite a fortune for a mere thrashing floor.

Though the building of the Temple was to be carried out by his son Solomon, David prepared cut stones and other materials, for Solomon was still very young. When his time came to pass away, David explained to his son what had happened, and gave him the *Tavnit*—scale model— that he was provided with in a divine vision, and indicated to him the selected place.

Solomon ascended the throne in Jerusalem—in the City of David— in 963 B.C. The Book of Kings states unequivocally that he began the construction of the Temple in the fourth year of his reign, completing it in the eleventh year, i.e., in 953 B.C. The festive inauguration of the

Temple took place once the Ark of the Covenant was installed in the Holy of Holies; Jewish traditions have always held that that most sacred spot was the rock on which Abraham was ready to sacrifice Isaac.

The construction of the Temple according to very detailed plans, I said to my group, is described in the Bible over many chapters. Measurements are given. Where the altar, the great basin, and other ritual compnents were located was recorded. But nowhere—nowhere!—is there any mention of the construction of the great platform on which the Temple, its courtyards, and its outer areas stood.

The only plausible explanation, I said, was that the platform was already there—the so-called "threshing floor." It is a sizable platform, artificially built, supported by retaining walls of astounding complexity and size. And if it existed there even before the Jebusites—we come to the issue of *who* had built it, and *why.*

And in understanding this crucial point, I said, we are ready for tomorrow's visit to the Temple Mount and to the incredible tunnel that runs along it on the west—the second tunnel of this tale of two tunnels.

✳✳✳

Postscript

SCIENTISTS BACK BIBLICAL TUNNEL. This was the headline on a news report, printed and broadcast worldwide at the beginning of September 2003. The news referred to a study, published in that week's issue of the scientific magazine *Nature,* in which three scientists reported that radiometric dating of the Silo'am Tunnel in Jerusalem confirmed that it was excavated at about 700 B.C. "or slightly earlier"—precisely the period of the reign of King Hezekiah.

The editors at *Nature* preceded the report (by scientists Amos Frumkin and Aryeh Shimron of Jerusalem, Israel, and Jeff Rosenbaum of Reading, England) with the observation that "The historical credibility of texts from the Bible is often debated when compared with Iron Age archaeological finds. . . . Here we report radiocarbon and U-Th dating of the Siloam Tunnel proving its Iron Age II date."

How nice to have biblical veracity reaffirmed!

14

ENIGMAS OF THE
TEMPLE WALLS

erra sancta, Holy Land.

Say the words, and everyone would immediately know that you are talking about that narrow sliver of earth between the Mediterranean Sea and the Jordan River, where pilgrims, for two millennia if not longer, have gone to evoke the past in the Land of the Bible.

Say *The Holy City,* and most everyone would immediately know that you are talking about Jerusalem. For centuries, Jerusalem has been depicted as the center of the world we call Earth (fig. 129) in conformity with one of its epithets, The Navel of the Earth.

In the Hebrew Bible (Old Testament), excluding references to the Hebrew God, Jerusalem's name appears more times than that of any other place or person's name. Its existence and its name are recorded in the annals of the kings of Assyria and Babylon, of Egyptian Pharaohs, of Greek and Roman rulers. It is first mentioned in the Bible in the tale of the War of the Kings (Genesis chapter 14), when the first Hebrew Patriarch, Abraham, pursued the invaders and retrieved their captives and booty; "and Malkizedek, the king of Shalem, a priest of the God Most High," came out to welcome the victorious Abraham with bread and wine, thanking Abraham for their return. That was about 4,000 years ago. Less than a century later, after the upheaval of Sodom and Gomorrah, Abraham returned to Jerusalem, but this time to its Mount

Figure 129

Moriah, ready to offer his beloved son Isaac as a sacrifice to God—a sacrifice turned down by the Angel of the Lord once Abraham's fealty was demonstrated. Four centuries or so later, when the Israelites entered Canaan at the end of the Exodus, it was Adonizedek, king of Jerusalem, who called upon the Canaanite city-kings to offer united resistance. But though the alliance was defeated, the Israelites refrained from seizing Jerusalem; the task fell to David, another four centuries later.

The ancient civilizations in whose records Jerusalem was mentioned are all gone. Ashur and Nineveh, Assyria's royal cities, are buried ruins. So is Babylon. So is Memphis, capital of ancient Egypt. Hattushash, the Hittite capital, is an archaeological site. The list of ancient capitals, to say nothing of lesser cities and towns that no longer exist, is long. Yet Jerusalem is still there in spite of wars, conquests, and destruction, still there and continuously inhabited.

The wonder increases as one realizes that all the other great cities of antiquity arose on the banks of a river, as a port on a seacoast, as a trading or defense outpost at major crossroads. Jerusalem is located where none of those requisites exist. It does not lie on the banks of a river—

indeed, its history is replete with a struggle to supply it with water. It is far from the seacoast. And the two major north–south routes of the Lands of the Bible, the Way of the Sea (Via Maris of the Romans) and the Way of the Kings, ran far from it—the first on the Mediterranean seacoast, the other east of the Jordan River. The east–west routes too ran well north and well south of Jerusalem.

It is not a place of natural resources: Gold, silver, copper have never been mined there. It lies in the midst of barren hills. So what was it that not only made it a place where men wished to live all those millennia, but also—already 4,000 years ago—caused its king to be regarded as a Priest of the God Most High?

And then, for at least the past 2,000 years, Jerusalem has been the Holy City?

So, in the very first briefing session after my group joined me and my wife in Jerusalem, I posed to them a simple yet provocative question: Why is Jerusalem a holy city, why is it sacred?

The answers, as expected, were simple. It was sacred to Christians because Jesus had preached there, because he spent his last days there with his twelve disciples, because he died there on the cross. The place was revered by Moslems because of the legend that one night their Prophet Mohammed was miraculously transported from Arabia to Jerusalem, to be taken aloft on a white horse to visit the prior saints in heaven. And it was sacred to Jews because that's where the Temple of Solomon stood and where its rebuilt Second Temple had stood.

Now, I asked the group, why was Jesus in Jerusalem to begin with? He was there because the Temple, the Jewish temple, was there. Why was Mohammed taken to Jerusalem, of all places, for the heavenly ascent, rather than be taken aloft from the Moslem holy city of Mecca? Because the Moslem holy book, the Koran, says that the takeoff had to be from the es-Shakra, the "Foundation Stone." It was the rock, according to tradition, where Abraham brought his son to be sacrificed on Mount Moriah, and on which the Temple's Ark of the Covenant was emplaced.

The Q & A session soon made clear that all three faiths revere Jerusalem because of the Temple; and that the focal point for all three has been the Temple Mount. The question to ponder, then, I said, is this: Why was the Temple built there, why is Mount Moriah the *Temple* Mount?

Having read my books, my group members knew where I was leading: to the conclusion that the great stone platform now called the

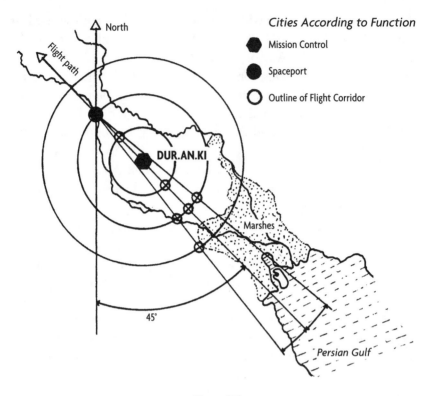

Figure 130

Temple Mount had already been there when David was divinely shown the scale model for the future temple; and that it has been there from way back, when the Anunnaki, after the Flood, chose that spot as their post-Diluvial Mission Control Center (see fig. 97, page 138)—taking over, in post-Diluvial times, the pre-Diluvial functions of Nippur (fig. 130) to serve as the DUR.AN.KI (the "Place of the Bond-Heaven-Earth"); that as Nippur had been, Jerusalem was the new center of concentrically placed space-flight sites, thus serving as the *Navel of the Earth.*

What the visit to Jerusalem intended to achieve, among the many other aspects of history, archaeology, and religions, was to find and see whatever evidence there was for my unorthodox conclusions regarding that space connection, of Jerusalem's role as the post-Diluvial Mission Control Center. The second tunnel of this tour, officially called the Western Wall Tunnel and commonly the Archaeological Tunnel, was where *such evidence existed, exposed for anyone to see.*

As it turned out, what was to be seen in this tunnel triggered another quest—an intensive inquiry might be more correct—for the disappeared Ark of the Covenant. I shall describe that experience in the final chapter of this book.

***

The Temple Mount, as visitors to it soon realize, is in fact a great horizontal stone platform erected atop Mount Moriah, which has a considerable natural slope from north to south (fig. 131). The levelness of the platform was achieved by both massive landfills and a series of floors resting on archways in the southern parts; all of that was kept from disintegrating and collapsing by the construction of retaining walls on all four sides of the platform.

The western side of the Temple platform extends for about 1,600 feet; the eastern side, due to the topography of the Mount, is somewhat shorter. The average east–west width is about 970 feet, so the platform represents a paved stone area of about 1,500,000 square feet; there is nothing comparable to it in the ancient Near East, with the exception of the even larger paved platform at Baalbek, Lebanon. At its maximum height, at the southwestern corner, the retaining wall—attributed to the time of the Second Temple—rises some 130 feet from rock bottom to its ancient top—i.e., not counting the later, topmost courses added in

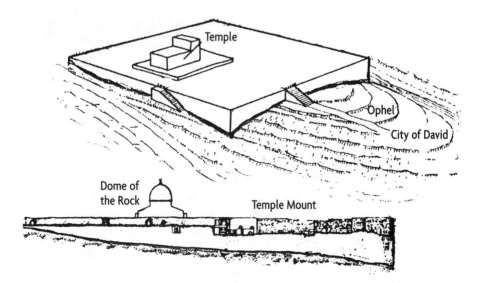

Figure 131

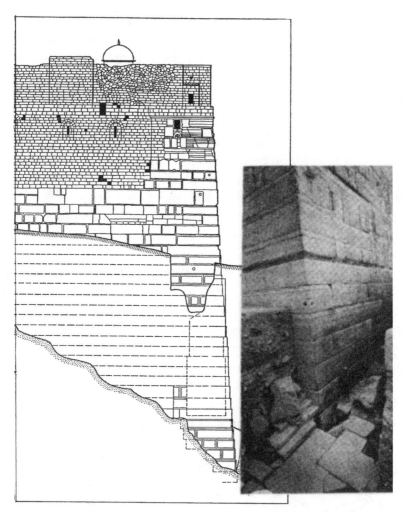

Figure 132

relatively recent centuries (fig. 132). At an average incline-height of 65 feet, we see here a landfill totaling more than 90 million cubic feet. Even allowing for the fact that some of the space under the platform is not solid fill or earth, but cavities, archways, and cisterns, the Temple platform represents a monumental feat of ancient construction.

Not all of this construction dates back to the very beginning; it is certain that King Herod (first century B.C.) added an extension to the original platform on the southern end, and a somewhat larger addition took place on the northern end. Still, at the beginning, and by Second Temple times, the platform had this shape and size—a mass of soil, partly artificially piled up, that had to be retained. That was the function of the retaining walls that surround the Temple Mount as a girdle.

These retaining walls were repaired, rebuilt, and extended over the millennia. But in their placement, and certainly in their lower courses, they belong to the platform's earliest times. The Western Wall, to which the Jews retained access even after the destruction of the Second Temple by the Romans in A.D. 70, is thus a remainder of the oldest structures of the Temple Mount. My group—and now the readers of this book— know that I believe it is some 12,000 years old . . .

It was King David who began, and his son Solomon who continued, to bridge the natural gap between the City of David and the unique platform to the north; the Bible refers to the area as the Milloh ("the Filling") or the Ophel ("the Climbing Up")—see fig. 120, page 183. The next step, under the kingship of Solomon, was to build the Temple. The Bible clearly states its purpose as that of creating a permanent home for the symbol of the Divine Presence, the Ark of the Covenant; and reinforces the link to the Exodus by stating that the building of the Temple began exactly 480 years after the beginning of the Exodus (I Kings 6:1). The construction lasted seven years; and in the year in which it was completed (taken to be 953 B.C.), on New Year's Day, according to the Jewish calendar, in full view of all the people, the priests carried the Ark of the Covenant "and brought it into the temple's *Dvir*, the Holy of Holies, and placed it under the wings of the Cherubim." And, the Bible added, "there was nothing in the Ark except the two stone tablets that Moses placed therein in the desert, when Yahweh had covenanted with the Children of Israel when they went out of Egypt."

While the Bible does not include an illustration of Solomon's Temple, sometimes referred to as the First Temple, the detailed written specifications have been the basis in modern times for artists' reconstructions and even scale-model reconstructions (and, as of 2002, even computer simulations). The accompanying illustration shows one of them (fig. 133). It is certain that the Temple was built along an east–west axis, its forecourts and main altar starting in the east and the Holy of Holies toward the west. As ancient temples go, it was thus an equinoctial temple, letting the sun's rays shine in precisely on equinox days. Sir Norman Lockyer, the father of the science of archaeoastronomy, called such temples Eternal Temples, because unlike Egyptian temples, which were oriented to the solstices, they did not require periodic reorientation due to changes in the Earth's tilt ("Precession").

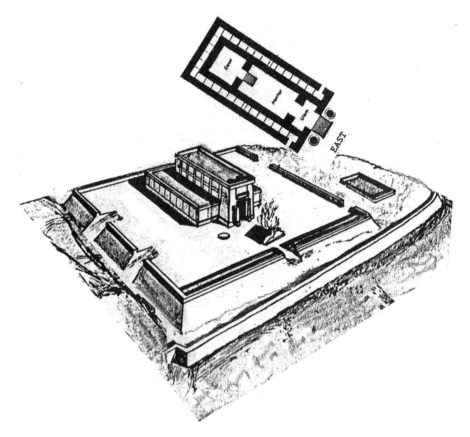

Figure 133

Where was the Holy of Holies—where was the Ark of the Covenant placed? Without exception, references in the writings of Jewish sages in post-biblical times and by historians such as Josephus Flavius suggest that it was upon the Foundation Stone (*Even Shatit* in Hebrew)—according to Jewish traditions the very rock on which Abraham placed Isaac to be sacrificed.

It is over that sacred rock that a Moslem Caliph, in the seventh century A.D., built the Dome of the Rock with its guilded dome—now the most prominent feature atop the Temple Mount, and one that dominates the Jerusalem skyline in the usual photographs of the city (plate 57). It is not a mosque; the mosque on the Temple Mount, called al-Aksa mosque, is situated at the southern end of the Temple platform, and was originally built by the Caliph Al-Walid in the eighth century A.D. (though as seen nowadays is primarily a rebuilding done in 1943). Jordan's King Abdallah was assassinated there by Palestinian extremists in 1951.

The Judean kingdom under David, and even more so under Solomon, embraced the original tribal Israelite lands and grew beyond that, expanding even as far as today's Baalbek in Lebanon and Damascus in Syria. With a richly built and decorated palace added to a gilded Temple, Jerusalem's fame and its king's wisdom spread to distant lands. Pharaohs gave their daughters as wives to Solomon, and the queen of Sheba (in southern Arabia, today's Yemen, and not in Ethiopia in Africa) paid a state visit.

Topography, especially the deep valley on the eastern side of the Temple Mount, channeled the growing population and its houses mostly to the west and northwest of the Temple Mount. When Nebuchadnezzar of Babylon attacked and sacked the city in the seventh century B.C., the enlarged Jerusalem was already protected by walls west and north of the Temple Mount. The returning exiles rebuilt and refortified the Temple and the city, giving rise to what is designated the Second Temple. Both the Temple and the city's walls were again restored after the Hashmonean revolt against Greek rule, in the second century B.C. Their successor, King Herod, conducted major and monumental building operations on the Temple Mount, in the access to it, and in the greater city itself.

The city that the Romans destroyed and burnt in 70 A.D., the city and Temple as Jesus knew them, already had the contours of what is nowadays called the Old City. Byzantines, Moslems, Crusaders, and, again, Moslems (who built the latest walls) left their mark mostly by the building of religious edifices—such as the Church of the Holy Sepulchre, which, according to Christian tradition, marks the place of the burial and resurrection of Jesus, and the Via Dolorosa, the street by which Jesus, carrying the cross, was led from the Antonia Fortress, where his trial and death sentence were issued by the Roman governor, to the place of the crucifixion.

Over the ensuing centuries the Jewish, Moslem, and Christian residents of the Old City congregated near and around their particular historic and sacred sites and houses of worship, establishing its division into the four quarters (fig. 134)—Jewish, Moslem, Armenian (i.e., Eastern Orthodox, stemming from Byzantium), and Christian (Catholic and other Christians). And the only way to see all that, and the Temple Mount too, is by walking, on foot . . .

With its people rammed into the confines of the walled area and ever

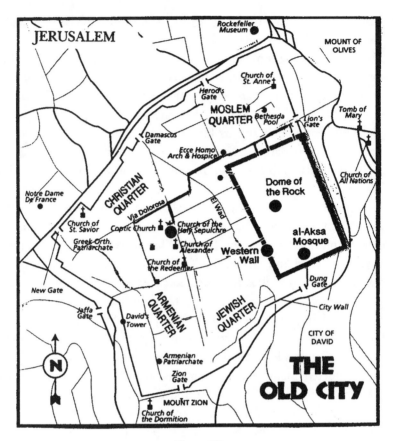

Figure 134

eager to live (and die) as close to the sacred locations as possible, the Old City of Jerusalem ended up as a multileveled place. I recall that the first time my wife and I took one of the eight guided walking tours available, we started at street level and after a while, walking on, we realized that we were walking on the rooftops of houses under our feet, where people lived and children played. At another time, walking among merchants' stalls in a narrow and winding street, we ended up below ground, at an excavated commercial street from Second Temple times. Everywhere, it seemed, as there was no more room available for new dwellings near the holy sites, buildings were built over or under other buildings, merging and mixing diverse periods.

The most significant of those multilevel, multiperiod walks was without doubt the one in the second tunnel of this Expedition's tale. Eager to live as close to the site of the Temples (First and Second) and ready to build one atop the other's house, the phenomenon of topping-over buildings reached its maximum as dwellings moved ever closer to the Western Wall. In earlier times—no one is sure when—a paved street ran along the length of the Western Wall. In time, as houses encroached and literally leant on the Wall, the street disappeared under the houses and whatever remained of it became tunnel-like. Only a very narrow portion of the Western Wall remained free of such encroachment, leaving a narrow stone-paved strip in front of it for prayers by Jews, who came there to bewail the Temples' destruction (hence the Wall's epithet, the "Wailing Wall"—fig. 135). During a visit in the nineteenth century, the explorer

Figure 135

Figure 136

Charles Wilson discovered that behind the wall and its doorway to the residence of the Moslem family charged with guarding the Western Wall, there were remains of an ancient arch (fig. 136). It supported a causeway that led to the Temple area from the Upper City and was the scene of one of the heroic stands against the Romans as told by Josephus.

Though the so-called Wilson's Arch attracted the attention of subsequent archaeologists, the full significance of what lay behind it did not come to light until after the 1967 Six Day War, when Israeli forces captured the Old City from the Jordanian Foreign Legion. In addition to clearing the encroaching structures to the south, exposing in time the complete length of the Western Wall in that direction, and creating the open plaza in front of it (plate 58), the Israeli authorities began to clear the "tunnel" in the northern direction. As debris was removed, it appeared that the space along the Wall continued northward, and was once upon a time an open-air street.

As slow progress was made, courses or levels of stonework and ashlars belonging to the Western Wall's full length came to view (though not to light), as well as adjoining chambers, halls, stairways, and passageways—a hidden maze that constituted an archaeological time machine.

By 1992, when my wife and I walked into and through this Western Wall Tunnel, it was sufficiently cleared and equipped with lighting, railings, and other safety features to allow very small groups to enter and explore it. The tunnel was not passable to its entire length, and the visitors had to turn back as they reached a certain point and retrace their steps, back to the entrance; this limited both the size of the visiting groups and their frequency. By the time my Earth Chronicles Expedition arrived in 1997, the tunnel had been opened through its full length; larger and more frequent groups were allowed in (though always by appointment, strictly enforced) and exit was made at the northern end, into the Via Dolorosa.

On the day designated for our tunnel appointment, the group entered the Old City through Jaffa Gate and its adjoining Tower of David, and walked the short distance to the Western Wall plaza. The lively conversations during the walk were replaced by silence as that remnant from Temple days rose up ahead, its numerous courses clearly distinguishable—larger ashlars, better fashioned, at the lower courses, smaller stone blocks less elaborately cut higher up. Jewish worshippers wearing prayer shawls filled the plaza. The group members approached the Wall as they wished, each one caught in his or her thoughts. I, as I have done before on numerous occasions, touched the sacred stones with my hands, then with my forehead, uttering a silent prayer. My wife, following a custom adhered to even by Pope John Paul II when he visited the site (fig. 137),

Figure 137

wrote down a prayerful wish on a piece of paper, then stuck the paper between the ashlars. Others in the group did the same. No one asked the other what he or she wished for. It was all an individual experience, a time for personal contemplation and reverence.

Regrouping, we walked to the southern edge of the plaza, where archaeological excavations were actively going on. Prior work exposed the southwestern corner of the Temple Mount's retaining wall, revealing how deep it went and how many courses of masonry there were below the assumed ground level (see fig. 132, page 202). Archaeologists also believe that there are sixteen (some say nineteen) courses below the plaza level where the Western Wall is exposed to the public. The sight at the south-western corner indicated both the massivity of the retaining walls and the immense engineering effort and challenge involved in filling up the slope and creating the flat horizontal platform on top. By comparison, the Filling from the time of David and Solomon that connected the City of David to the Temple Mount looked primitive.

Our Tunnel appointment time neared, and we moved toward the Tunnel's entranceway. It was not, as one would have assumed, through Wilson's Arch, but at an opening to the west of it, reachable by stairs. The way in then passes through high-ceilinged chambers, narrow passageways leading eastward; then, a sharp turn to the left is made and one finds one-self in another world. Dimly lit signs flank a wide stairway down several flights, where a wall of immense stone blocks comes into view, through an ancient archway (plate 59).

Before going down to the actual "tunnel," the group settled on benches in a cavernlike opening, facing a three-dimensional model of the Temple Mount, showing how houses encroached on the Western Wall. The assigned guide explained various features of the place and its struc-tures, then pressed a button and the display's forepart and the encroach-ments sank into an unseen cavity and the full length of the Wall, as it is now known to have been, appeared into unobstructed view. It was then my turn to take the microphone, and I prepared the group for the soon-to-be-seen incredible sight. In the wall facing us down the stairs there are placed four colossal—and I mean *colossal,* I said—stone blocks the likes of which there are none anywhere else in the Near East, including Egypt and its pyramids, except at Baalbek in Lebanon.

Thus forewarned, the group left the benches and went down the stairs. The passageway in front of the Western Wall section exposed there was too narrow to allow a proper photographic perspective for capturing the immensity of those stone blocks, all perfectly shaped with smooth faces. (On a previous visit I positioned my wife at the end of one stone block and our personal guide at its other end to show how long the stone block was—see plate 60). The blocks make up a 127-foot-long section of the Wall. They are an extraordinary eleven feet high, about double the height of the already unusually high stone blocks in the course below it (fig. 138).

One of the four stone blocks, which have been dubbed the Master Course of the Western Wall, is a staggering 46 feet long, a length that we tried to connote by having about a dozen of our group stand in front of it (plate 61). Its width (or depth) was determined by soil-penetrating radar to be 14 feet. This immense size translates into a weight of almost 600 tons. The stone block next to it is almost identical, at a length of 40 feet. The third is shorter, at 35 feet, but of the same height and width. The fourth stone block that completes this section is a mere six feet long, still weighing almost 90 tons, which is about five times the largest limestone block in the Giza pyramids (where the common stone blocks weigh

Figure 138

a mere 2.5 tons) and more than twice the largest stone in Stonehenge, England.

The Master Course, as heavy as its stone blocks are, is not placed upon solid ground. It rests upon another course of larger than usual stone blocks, at the level of the pavement that forms the tunnel's floor. But that too is not true ground level; excavations and probes have suggested that there are other courses below the pavement, perhaps as many as thirteen; that translates to some seventy more feet of Wall going down. True ground level, where the Wall rests on the native rock, runs at a slope from north (higher) to south (lower). Archaeologists have determined that under the street that the tunnel uses there ran another, earlier street that followed the natural incline; indeed, the remains of such a street meet the current floor at a point farther north.

That we were not walking at true ground level became clear as we left the colossal stone blocks and moved on. Openings, sometimes covered with wood flooring or steel sheets and sometimes with heavy Plexiglas so that what was below could be seen, were encountered all along the tunnel. While to the right as we walked, the Wall and its ashlars continued, to the left there were cavernlike open spaces, remains of structures, decorated columns, parts of stairs and stairwells. Special illuminated signs identified the remains here and there, indicating that we were seeing the evidence of the past, a kind of Jerusalem-through-the-ages gallery beginning with the era of the Judean kings, then the various conquerors and destroyers—Babylonian, Roman, Byzantine: a Hellenistic period, a Hashmonaean period, a Herodian period; Crusader remains, Moslem remains.

To see it all in the darkness or semi-darkness, with one period not just above another but mixed in with others, was like walking on another planet and seeing the remains of its civilizations. It was like watching a history movie, but being part of and within the movie. It was, in short, like traveling in a time machine.

At one spot, reached just after the four colossal stone blocks, everyone that walked by was jarred. There, as part of the wall, without doubt, was an arched doorway, now blocked by masonry. Signs announced that here was *an entranceway that aligned directly with the Holy of Holies of the Temple!* (Fig. 139 and plate 62.) We were at the heart of the Temple enigmas.

Since we were dozens of feet below the level of the Temple platform, there had to be a stairway leading up from this arched entranceway (also known as Warren's Gate in honor of the nineteenth-century explorer who

Figure 139

explored and mapped the various cisterns and caverns under the Temple Platform). Experts in Second Temple reconstructions that follow Temple descriptions from the time believe that there had to be in the northern section of the western wall a gateway matching the one to the south, the so-called Barclay's Gate. Indeed, Warren indicated the existence of a cavern connected via a secret passage to the gateway (fig. 140); if it duplicated the southern Barclay's Gate, it would provide a secret way up to the Temple!

What lies behind this gateway, just beyond the colossal Master

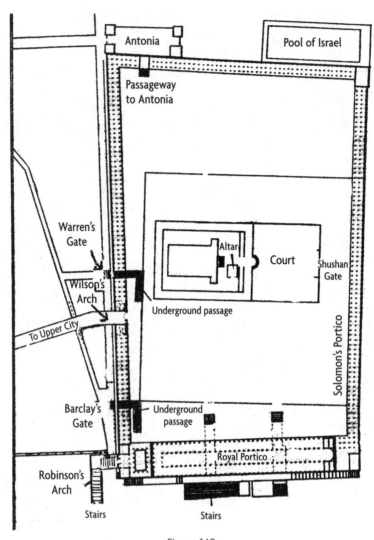

Figure 140

Course? For religious and political reasons, Warren's Gate has not been breached; but radar, ultrasound, and other devices indicate that there is a substantial cave or cavity behind it. If it is a northern twin of the more southerly "Barclay's Gate," then it might have, as does the southern one, an L-shaped secret passage eastward, which then turns at a ninety-degree angle, leading up to the Temple courtyards. Did the entranceway lead to a passageway that turned at once southward, to connect to the cavity behind the colossal blocks, rather than run first eastward (as the Barclay passage does, for 84 feet) and then turn in an L-shape? That is a very intriguing question that will remain unresolved as long as present political-religious circumstances continue.

How old is this entranceway to the innermost parts of the Temple Mount? Most archaeologists date it, as well as the other four western wall entranceways (see fig. 140), to King Herod's time. But in some instances, such as in the case of Wilson's Arch, the evidence suggests that Herod's architects and builders used *earlier* entranceway components. Could the now blocked gateway in the Tunnel have existed from the time of the First Temple?

One Jewish tradition, deemed by scholars more legend than fact, tells that this entranceway in the western wall was a secret way to the Temple Mount used by King David. Since the Temple was not built yet in his time, and if the legend has some basis in fact, then he must have had another reason to use the entranceway for going up. To the enigmatic "threshing floor"?

In spite of the Tunnel's confines and the mingling of other groups into ours, I pointed here and showed there those enigmatic features. I stressed the puzzling proximity of this gateway to the colossal stone blocks. It has been established that there is a large cavity behind the blocks. Did it connect to the Holy of Holies?

This mysterious gateway-passageway, placed right next to the Master Course, may hold the answer to the question: What was the purpose of these colossal stone blocks? But meanwhile, it only redoubles the enigma . . .

There, in the semi-darkness of the subterranean tunnel, "We are witnessing remains from the earliest period, when the Anunnaki, and not kings, created the Platform and established upon it their Mission Control Center," I told my group. I suggested that we could find more evidence when we went up the Mount again.

The Tunnel extends for about 1,000 feet in total, and there was much more to see and feel bewitched by as we walked on; but the pressure of other groups behind us increased, and we had to keep moving with the crowd. At the northern end of the Tunnel, a newly installed metal staircase leads up to an exit on the Via Dolorosa. The exit has a metal door outside that is indistinguishable from the front doors of adjoining houses; save for an Israeli guard outside, one could not even know that this is the Tunnel's exit. Yet it took years to get the Moslem authorities to consent to the exit, and bloody riots followed its opening in spite of that.

Figure 141

As planned, the group followed the Via Dolorosa, the "Street of Sorrows." It is now completely commercialized, save for the markers set in the walls indicating the Stations of the Cross (fig. 141). The destination was the Church of the Holy in the Christian Quarter (fig. 142); the visit to this unique shrine lasted about an hour. From there we took teeming side streets to reach the excavated and now open to the air *Cardo,* the main north–south colonnaded street of Jerusalem at the time of the Second Temple, the time of Jesus and the Roman rule. We stopped for refreshments and a quick lunch.

It was time, our guide said, to return to the Western Wall Plaza and go up to the Temple Mount Platform itself.

***

Before describing the experiences there, let me report briefly the gist of the group's discussions that evening concerning the Tunnel.

Apart from personal observations by the participants of how they felt at the Western Wall and inside the Tunnel, the principal focus was on the Master Course and its colossal stone blocks. How were they brought to the Tunnel, how were they placed, by whom, and for what purpose?

Figure 142

I mentioned that trying to explain how this or that king might have done it, Israeli archaeologists have suggested that the stone blocks were first cut as cylinders that could be rolled on the ground, and thus brought from the quarry (some say two miles, some say five miles away); then, the curvatures were hewn off to create the right-angled ashlars. But it was pointed out that the giant cylinders would have weighed almost double the ashlars' weight, that the idea that the stones were rolled over hills and valleys did not make sense, and that cutting the stones to shape at the Temple site went against the strict biblical assertion that no stone cutting with iron tools could take place at the site—all the stone blocks for Solomon's Temple, the Bible clearly states, were precut.

Another idea offered by some archaeologists was that the stone blocks, precut at the quarry site, were then lifted and placed on smoothed wooden logs that served as rollers, then pulled on those wooden rollers (by men or even oxen) to the site of the Wall. In response to that, I pointed out to the group that 600 tons equaled the weight of thirty Cadillacs. Imagine, I said, thirty Cadillacs piled up on wooden logs, and workers trying to keep that rolling . . .

As impractical as such solutions were, they also left completely unanswered the question of *who* in antiquity was capable of lifting such weighty stone blocks and putting them precisely in place *above* another row ("course") of stone blocks. Even less touched upon by those theories was the question, *Why* were these stones placed here?

No matter how much we tried to play the archaeologists' advocate, the only clues seemed to come from the similarities between this site and Baalbek. Both have, in the retaining western wall, three colossal stone blocks (the Trilithon at Baalbek), placed upon another course of unusually large stone blocks, held in place over millennia without mortar or cement, quarried some distance away and lifted and carried into place.

We concluded it could only be the handiwork of the Anunnaki.

And this could well be the case, if I was right in suggesting that Jerusalem, serving as Mission Control Center, was linked to Baalbek ("The Landing Place") as part of the post-Diluvial Landing Corridor.

There's one more thing, I said when we finally called it a day, and my group got up to leave. It may or may not be an important clue: The caliph who built the Dome of the Rock brought its gilded dome from Baalbek, where it used to top the mosque there . . .

15

SECRETS OF THE
SACRED ROCK

Having journeyed through tunnels and other subterranean mar-
vels of ancient Jerusalem (there was much more encompassed in
five days than thus far described), the Expedition group was
looking forward to visiting what was on top—the Temple Platform in
bright sunlight. There was indeed much there to satisfy curiosity, a search
for history, a quest for spiritual origins. We were about to see with our
own eyes and experience with all of our being the holy site of the Temple,
the Sacred Rock; the spot where history, religions, nationalism—and
according to me, the presence of the Anunnaki—converge.

But unrevealed to my group was yet another target that I had secretly
in mind: *to explore the underbelly of the Sacred Rock and find a clue to the
mystery of the vanished Ark of the Covenant.* To attempt that could have
involved daredevil situations, and there was no need, I felt, to involve the
whole group in that . . .

Getting up to the Temple Mount was, by itself, not a cut-and-dried
matter. After Israel took control of the Old City in the 1967 Six Day War,
it left to the Moslem Wakf (Religious Sites Trust) much autonomy to
administer the Temple Platform and the Moslem structures on it. On
Fridays (the Moslem prayer day) and other Moslem holidays, Moslems
retained unlimited access to the Temple Mount from its northern gates,
where the platform reaches the level of the Moslem Quarter of the Old

City. All others, which means primarily Jews and Christians, were provided with access via a ramp abutting the Western Wall. From time to time rioting by Arabs on the Temple Mount or Arab-Israeli clashes elsewhere would cause the non-Moslem access to be halted, temporarily or for longer periods. The Earth Chronicles Expedition to the Holy Land was so timed by me as to take place at a relatively tranquil respite.

To understand what access or ascent to the Temple Mount means, and to understand what one sees or can expect to see, one needs a brief history lesson. I provided it to my group in extensive Briefing Notes, a thick folder that each participant received, containing information discussed and enlarged upon in daily Briefing Sessions.

Towering above its surroundings on all sides except the north, the Temple Mount requires an ascent to reach its hallowed platform with its present and past sacred shrines. As commanded by the Lord (the book of Exodus), Jewish males were required to go up—ascend—to Jerusalem three times a year, on the festivals of Tabernacles, Pentecost, and Passover. The location of the City of David and Jerusalem's growth under the Judean kings (see fig. 120, page 183, and fig. 131, page 201) leave no doubt that the access for the ascending pilgrims was from the south; indeed, the earthworks named in the Bible as the Milloh ("Filling") and Ophel ("Rising, Ascent") might have been undertaken in order to enable the multitudes to reach the Temple that Solomon built. That southern access was enlarged and made more monumental in Second Temple times (fig. 143).

That First Temple was destroyed by Nebuchadnezzar, the Babylonian king, in 587 B.C. Seventy years later the Persian king Cyrus, who captured Babylon and ended its mighty empire, permitted the Judean exiles to return and rebuild the Jerusalem Temple. Whether it was rebuilt exactly as it once was or in accordance with the plans revealed to the Prophet Ezekiel in a holographic vision, no one can say for certain. That Second Temple was enhanced, defiled, and purified repeatedly when Greeks followed Persians as masters of the Near East. The Purification of the Temple and the resumption of Jewish kingship under the Hashmonaeans in 164 B.C. served as a prelude for the major reconstruction works by King Herod (37 B.C. to 4 B.C.). The city (fig. 143) and the glorious Second Temple, as described by historians of the time (fig. 144)—the time of Jesus and Roman rule—was by then the scene of tens of thousands of pilgrims at the three Ascent festivals, and especially during Passover.

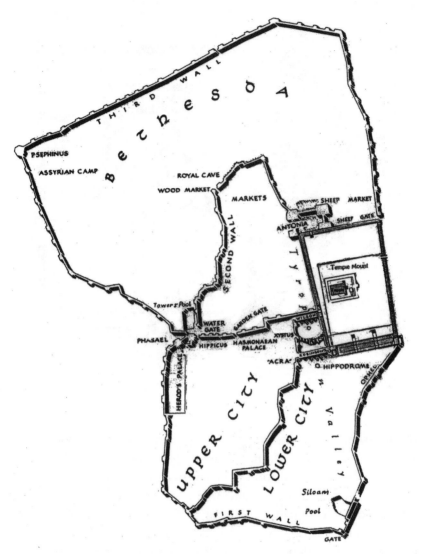

Figure 143

Records from the time and archaeological excavations confirm that the main public access to the Temple Platform was from the south, where monumental stairs led to five gates (fig. 145); open air as well as underground passageways led the pilgrims to the various courtyards of the Temple proper. It was at that area that money changers—not money lenders, as is commonly believed—had their stalls, because the foreign coins bearing images of the Roman emperors (fig. 146) had to be

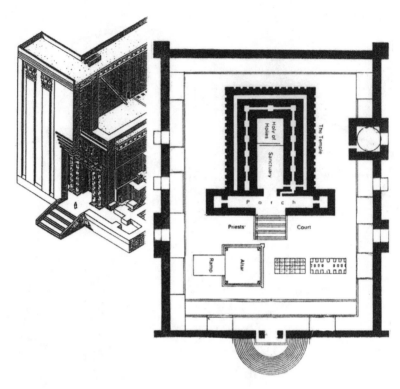

Figure 144

exchanged for local coins that bore no graven images of people. It was there that the preacher from Nazareth, Jesus, overturned the money changers' tables as described in the New Testament.

The king, the noblemen, and the priests, however, had their special entryway to the Temple Platform from the west, where the newer sections were. A great stairway was constructed, running first from south to north, and then, supported by a massive archway, provided a west–east set of stairs for entering the Temple Mount via a monumental columned gate (fig. 147). Only the upper part of its archway, still attached to the western wall, is still extant; it is called Robinson's Arch, after its nineteenth-century discoverer.

Somewhat to its north, still in the Western Wall, a less monumental and probably much older gateway existed, reached by a number of functional stairs now called Barclay's Gate, after its discoverer, also in the nineteenth century (fig. 148). Blocked off, it is now almost completely obscured by the current way to ascend to the Temple Platform, which

Figure 145

Roman coin of Titus   Roman coin of Vespasian

Jewish shekel

Figure 146

Figure 147

Figure 148

follows the architectural plan of the stairway from the time of the Second Temple. In reality, a simple earthen ramp improved with steps (fig. 149), it leads from the level of the Western Wall Plaza up to the level of the Temple Platform through what is simply and prosaically called the Green Door. And that's how I and my fans went up to the Temple Mount that day.

The walk up starts near the southern end of the Western Wall, where it makes a ninety-degree angle with the southern retaining wall. Israeli archaeologists have been excavating there, exposing the majestic portions of the retaining walls that had been hidden for millennia. The excavations confirmed what had been assumed: that there are as many courses below current ground level as there are above it (see fig. 132, page 202). The excavators found there a jumble of toppled ashlars; small finds (like coins) confirmed the theory that the ashlars down there were toppled by Roman soldiers as they systematically destroyed the Temple and its walls in the first century A.D. Linking that corner with the cleared area along the southern wall, where the monumental stairway and arched gates have been uncovered, the Israelis created an archaeological park, with its own small museum. We lingered there long enough to take photographs and wonder again at the immensity of the retaining walls of the Temple

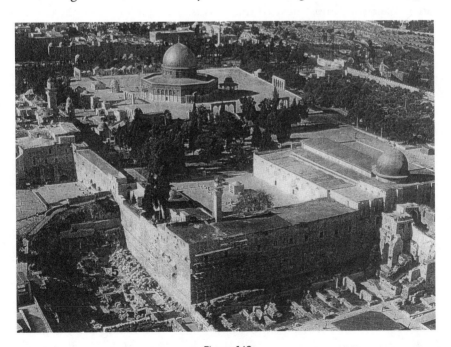

Figure 149

Mount. Urged by our guide to start the ascent to the Temple Platform, we never really examined this remarkable site.

A small booth manned by several Israeli policemen stood at the end of the ramp, near the Green Door. As we approached the door, two of the policemen emerged to ask us some questions, mainly who we were, from where, and why were we coming up. Selectively, they asked to see passports. It seemed odd to them that there were two Canadians and one Japanese among the presumed group of American tourists. We were all wearing the special Earth Chronicles Tours white hats, and they wondered why mine was blue. In what appeared to be an offhanded, nonchalant questioning, they evaluated us quite professionally. Their purpose? To make sure there were no "troublemakers" among us.

Passing the Israeli test was not the end of it. No sooner had we passed through the doorway and onto the great stone platform than we were met by casually dressed Moslem men who represented themselves as tour guides but who in effect kept us near the entrance and oh-so-casually bombarded us with their questions. In the end it seemed that the size of our group (over thirty) and the fact that more than half were women ("womans" to them) bothered them.

The entrance, through the Green Door, gets the visitor to an open-air passageway almost next to the Al-Aqsa mosque on the right (to the south); the Dome of the Rock stands, on a higher platform, farther to the left (northward). As some of us wandered off to the right, the Arab guides—actually guards employed by the Wakf—hurriedly blocked their way. No mosque! No mosque! they shouted.

It was becoming clear that we would not be allowed to freely roam over the majestic platform, so we pressed to be allowed to see the Dome of the Rock. You must wait, the guides/guards said, it is now the prayer hour. That was odd, since the Dome of the Rock is not a mosque, but there was no point in arguing. Where we remained waiting, trees provided a pleasant shade. It seemed odd, or better said unexpected, to see trees all the way up here, so many courses up from true ground level. As we broke ranks and milled about, it seemed even odder that the trees—at some spots quite densely growing together—appeared to grow all around, *except* on the extra-raised platform on which the Dome of the Rock stood (fig. 150). Was there anything about the sacred Rock that kept trees away? I wondered out loud, pointing out the phenomenon to the group.

In spite of the tension engendered by the questioning and the delay, there was a remarkable tranquillity to the place. With hardly anyone

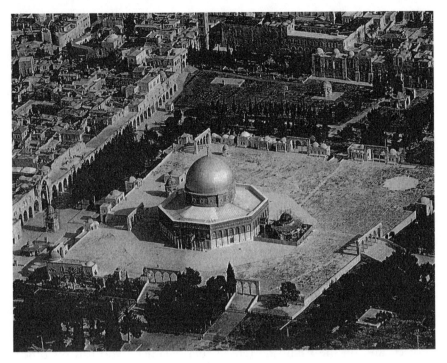

Figure 150

about the platform except us and our "hosts," a quiet serenity embraced the place. Although it was the hottest time of the day, we felt a cool breeze. We well knew that there were days here of riots and stone throwing, at Israeli policemen and at worshippers below at the Western Wall, but that day it was peaceful, tranquil, quiet.

The city that once was, in antiquity, and the teeming city that Jerusalem is today, were all around the Temple Mount; yet their sounds did not reach here. Church towers and towering high-rises reared their heads as one looked west, north; the Mount of Olives, with its accumulation of tombstones, beckoned to the east. There were roads below, traffic, praying crowds, haggling merchants. But here, on that day, there was a silent tranquillity. I could not recall where exactly in the Bible it was stated that God makes his presence known in a serene silence, but that is what I was thinking, that is what I was feeling, that day at that time on the Temple Mount.

My thoughts came back to reality as I wondered what was delaying us from proceeding to the Dome of the Rock. Other groups, I was told beforehand, had had no problem. Was there anything different about our group, or, as Israeli experience had taught, were the Moslems conducting some digging or other work they didn't wish others to see?

As we were waiting and waiting, it was time to unleash my "secret weapon," I thought to myself. I got hold of one of the guide/guards. "Where is the office of Dr. Khader Salameh?" I asked him." I want to see Dr. Salameh!"

"You know Dr. Salameh?" the man responded, surprised. "Yes, yes!" I said impatiently. "He knows me, we corresponded, I telephoned him! I want to see him!" Though exaggerated, my statement was essentially true. One of my fans, Joseph Peeples of Texas, was the president of the Jerusalem Historical Society, an entity established by him to facilitate research into the history and prehistory of Jerusalem. He was also the founder of the Christian Origins Library, which was publishing scholarly works in the fields of theology and archaeology. He had come to New York to meet me many times, seeking my help for his book, *The Destruction of Jerusalem*. On his frequent stays in Israel, he befriended Dan Bahat, the Israeli archaeologist in charge of the Western Wall Tunnel project, and on the Arab side Dr. Khader Salameh, who had his office right there on the Temple Mount. Unable to come along on this Expedition, Mr. Peeples had advised both Bahat and Salameh of my impending visit, asked that I be given all possible assistance, and provided me with copies of this correspondence, addresses, and telephone numbers. Dr. Bahat was out of the country, but Dr. Salameh was in town, and I had left him telephone messages that I was there, and at what hotel. He did not call back, but that was no reason not to wave his name to the guide/guards . . .

Given my name, the man I spoke to hurried to one of the one-story buildings that hugged the Platform's circumference, but came back with the news that Dr. Salameh was not in the office and was not expected back until later in the day. My acquaintance with Dr. Salameh seemed to break the ice all the same. In my own mind I began to mull over how I could manage to achieve what I was really after: to find a way to go *under* the sacred rock, where a cavelike space exists. Virtually every traveler and explorer in past centuries reported and depicted such a cavity (fig. 151), and some suggested that under that one there was yet another hidden one. Count Melchior de Vogüé, who explored the site in the nineteenth century, even reported a second sub-cavity connected to others by a tunnel (fig. 152).

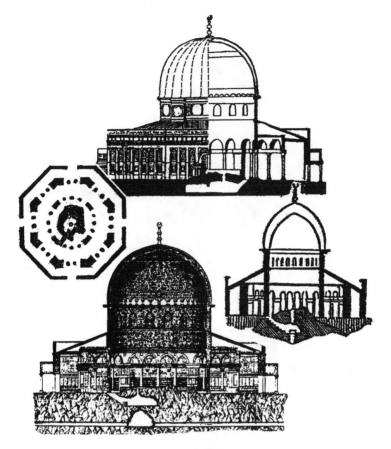

Figure 151

During previous Expeditions, when a museum would not allow photographing, our group would congregate and huddle at a certain exhibit so that one of us, hidden from the museum guards, could still take a picture. Now I considered how we could perhaps create such a cover for a quick look down inside the Dome of the Rock . . .

But those plans were soon dashed. After more consultations at the Dome by our "hosts," word came back that we could proceed to visit the Dome—but would have to enter it only in small groups, and no cameras! Left with no other choice, we proceeded to the Dome of the Rock, taking many pictures outside (plate 63).

The Dome of the Rock, an eight-sided building capped by the famed gilded dome, rests on a platform of paved stones that rises many feet over

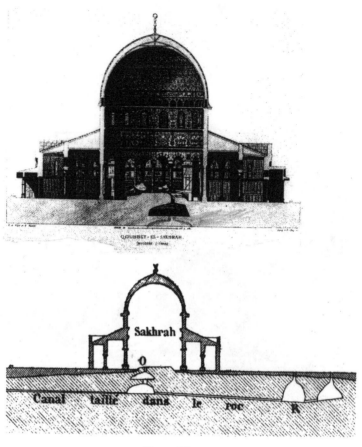

Figure 152

and above the larger general Temple Mount platform, and is reached by going up any one of several staircases via arches simulating gates (fig. 150, page 227). Archaeologists and biblical scholars have been debating whether that second platform belongs to the First or to the Second Temple period, but with few exceptions they agree that this second raised platform was there during Temple times and is not a post-Temple feature. One reason for that conclusion is the historically recorded fact that, certainly in Second Temple times, the Temple was reached by twelve steps coming from the general platform. Another is that an adjoining round building called the Dome of the Chain (see fig. 150, page 227) appears to stand where the Great Altar stood in Temple times. The most plausible explanation for the second raised platform is that it raised the Temple's ground level to a height that matched the level of the top of the Sacred Rock—

enabling to position there, on a level floor, the Ark of the Covenant.

The Dome of the Rock's walls, inside and outside, are covered with calligraphed verses from the Koran, the Moslem holy book; and some researchers have pointed out that, curiously, none of the proliferation of verses includes those that pertain to Mohammed's nighttime ascent to heaven from this very Sacred Rock. This fact is taken by some to indicate that the real reason for the erection of the Dome, starting in the seventh century A.D., was the association of the Rock with the Temple's Holy of Holies.

There had been no doubt in my mind, as indicated in the Briefing Notes that were prepared for the group, that in entering the Dome of the Rock we would enter the site of the Holy of Holies, and that the Rock is where the Ark of the Covenant had once stood (fig. 153). As my group and readers knew, I took the sacredness further back in time, to when the site was the Navel of the Earth, the Mission Control Center of the Anunnaki in post-Diluvial times. The colossal stone blocks of the Master Course discovered in the Western Wall Tunnel, akin to the Trilithon in Baalbek, strengthened that conviction, and the secret gateway (Warren's Gate) and

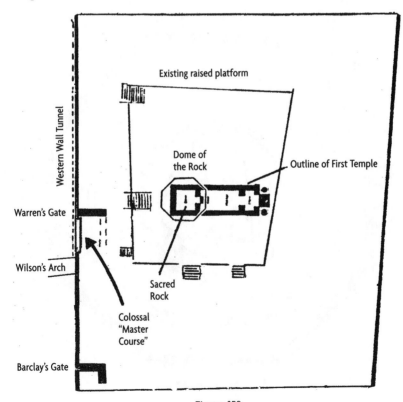

Figure 153

its presumed tunnel into and up to the site of the Holy of Holies opened up tantalizing possibilities regarding the fate of the Ark of the Covenant.

Thus believing (or indoctrinated), the group reached the Dome's visitors' entrance. Taking off our shoes and leaving cameras behind, we were let in six or seven at a time. I went in with the first group and remained inside until all the others had had a chance to come in and hear my semi-whispered explanations.

The interior of the Dome of the Rock is an impressive columned and colorful structure encircling the Sacred Rock (called as-Sakhra, "Foundation Rock," in Arabic). The outer octagonal wall encircles two inner concentric cloisters that support the inclined inner ceiling inside of the dome. Colored light shines in through the stained-glass windows that encircle an ornamented structural girdle under the dome itself. They let light in, filtered through the stained glass, and thus add to the medley of colors and the play of light and shadows inside the Dome of the Rock.

The first inner ring of columns (fig. 154) follows the outer octagonal

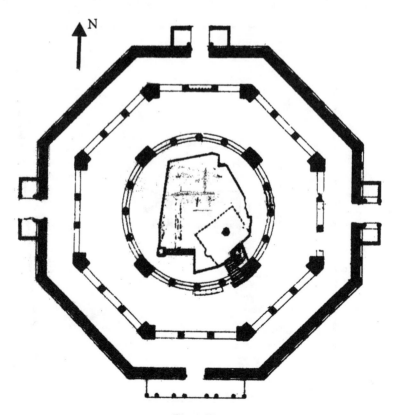

Figure 154

contour; the inner colonnade, circular in shape, provides sixteen supporting arches between two pillars and three columns on each of four segments. White marble, blue tiles, gilded inscriptions, and red carpets provide the dominant hues. Combined with the colored rays of light and a wealth of artistic details, they all somehow manage to focus, rather than distract, attention on the extraordinary natural rock that is the center of all that effort (plate 64).

There are carpets on the floor surrounding the Rock to absorb the sound of footsteps; and though there are no signs requiring silence, we all spoke softly or even in whispers, instinctively feeling that loud talking would seem inappropriate. A wooden parapet and railings surround the Rock, and a small viewing stand has been provided from which visitors can gaze upon it. The Sacred Rock is quite a massive stone outcropping, measuring some fifty by forty feet. Its face, as is apparent in photographs (fig. 155 and fig. 156), bears markings of various fashionings and cuttings that created both smooth flat areas as well as niches upon the Rock. When these were made no one can say, although some are attributed to the Crusaders, who chipped off pieces of the Rock and sold them to Christian pilgrims. If that is where the Temple's Holy of Holies was and where the Ark of the Covenant was placed, the fashionings, some showing right angles, make sense.

Figure 155

Figure 156

Most intriguing to Bible scholars is the straight or straightened western side of the Rock, made even more prominent by the balustrade that runs along it and that makes perfect right angles with the shorter railings on the two connecting sides. The south face of the Rock there suggests that the straight line had to be artificially created. A leading student of Solomon's Temple, the Dutch archaeologist Leen Ritmeyer, has concluded that this straight side of the Rock matches exactly the western side of the Holy of Holies.

To the right of the visitors' stand one can see a perfectly round hole that was bored or cut through the Rock (fig. 155). The hole is about two feet in diameter. Cleanly cut through some six or seven feet of solid rock, it is a technological feat whose purpose, time, and perpetrator remain a mystery. It is not located in the center of the Rock or even near it, so why is it there? I was asked. I said I didn't know, and know of not even a theory offered by anyone else.

Between the viewing stand and the location of the hole are the stairs that lead down to the Rock's underbelly, the cave or cavern that intrigued me so much. That was where I wanted to go, but there was no way to achieve it then and there.

Since the guards who were watching us (though we did not always notice them) did not object, we walked around the Rock to view it from all sides. Seen from such different view lines, features on the face of the Rock, unnoticed from one side, came into view from the other, evoking excited whispers of Look at that! Look at this! We slowed down as we passed by the stairs leading down into the cavern. It was too dim inside to see it clearly. I wondered whether I should dash down while walking with one group, then reemerge when the other group's turn came. But the watchful guards made the idea just wishful thinking, and I did not dare.

With no cameras and with other group members waiting outside each time, I felt that the visit to the Dome of the Rock fell short of my expectations. But the others with me felt exhilarated, even awed by the physical proximity to the venerated and hallowed relic.

According to the traditions and beliefs of three faiths, we were at the Navel of the Earth, seeing with our own eyes the great and sacred Foundation Stone, standing where Abraham was tested, where the Holy of Holies of Solomon's Temple was, where in Temple days only the High Priest could enter to face the Ark of the Covenant. And all that, in spite of the wait, the guards, and the hurried atmosphere, was cause for exhilaration, exuberance, reverence.

***

We were leaving the Temple Mount and almost at the Green Door exit when the guide/guard with whom I had spoken before caught up with us. Dr. Salameh is back in his office and you can see him now, he said.

After some consulting it was decided that while I went and met Dr. Salameh, there was no point in holding up the group, and the others went ahead with the day's sightseeing program while I and my wife were led to the Wakf offices.

We were greeted by Dr. Salameh at the entrance to his office with a warm handshake. "Please, please come in, be seated!" he invited us. The narrow office was crammed with books. "Your office reminds me of mine," I said, "books, books, books . . ." We were asked if we would have tea, and when we said yes, a male attendant brought in three cups on a tray of polished copper, pouring the sweet tea from a beaked teapot, also made of copper. We praised the sweet tea and spent some time talking about our mutual friend, Joseph Peeples. The praise bestowed on him and his Jerusalem Historical Society suggested to me that some contribution(s) to Dr. Salameh's endeavors or library must have been made, and I felt obliged to show great curiosity about the books lining the walls and piled up on the desk of Dr. Salameh. The books, I must confess, included some that made me envious.

Finally, politely as befits longtime friends, he came around to the purpose of my coming up to the Mount. I described my work and writings as dealing with ancient civilizations and the origins of religions—a subject, I said, which he will agree must include the site venerated by Islam, Christianity, and Judaism (in that order). "I am fascinated by the Sacred Rock," I said. "A pity that my group could not take a good look at it, nor take pictures. Could I come back and do that?"

He talked awhile around the subject, then said that I surely understand that "these days" great care must be taken in allowing "sensitive things." He would have liked to help me, but the most he could do was act as a conduit for submitting an application by me—a written application—to the Wakf authorities "higher up." "How long will it take to get approval?" I asked. "Oh, I will try to get it for you in two weeks," he said.

"I will not be here in two weeks," I said. "How about a week? I can then come back to the Mount at the end of our stay in the country." He gestured, indicating "Who knows?" I said that I would see how my plans to stay went, and thus would call him if I decided to apply.

We parted most cordially, with nothing much achieved. "It didn't work," I said to my wife. "At least the tea was good," she said.

Outside the office building, the persistent guide/guard was awaiting us. "How did it go?" he asked. I told him what I had asked for and the answer I received.

He stared at me, as if trying to penetrate my inner workings. "Can you come back tomorrow, at ten o'clock?" he asked. I looked back at him. "Yes, I can," I said. "So come back tomorrow—by yourself!" He added, "I will wait for you at this entrance."

I asked for his name. "Mahmoud, they call me Mahmoud!" he said. We shook hands. As I turned to walk away, he kept holding my hand. "Bring cash," he said in a half-whisper; "no traveler's checks."

As we came down the ramp, my wife stated as a question: "You are not going tomorrow?"

"Oh yes, I am!" I said.

∗∗∗

At breakfast next morning—the buffet breakfasts at Israeli hotels are a sumptuous and leisurely affair—I discussed the day's program with the tour leader and the tour guide and re-arranged some of the plans so as to keep the group busy between ten and twelve without me. I then decided to take into my confidence Wally M., a veteran of some of the previous expeditions and a genius at managing to take pictures where none are supposed to be taken. He readily agreed to give up the morning's tour in order to go back with me to the Mount.

"Didn't the man say that you should come by yourself?" my wife asked. "Yes, he did," I said, "but what he meant was Not With A Woman."

Wally and I were at the Green Door promptly at 10:00 A.M., and Mahmoud was there waiting for us. He led us quickly to the entrance of the Dome of the Rock, and as we stood aside held a lively conversation with a heavyset man at the entrance. Then Mahmoud came back to us. "Two people OK," he said, "but only one camera." He quoted a number, meaning so many Israeli shekels. "You are not serious?" I countered, trained in the Middle East's ways of bargaining. "He has to share it," Mahmoud explained, pointing with a nod to the heavyset man. I hand-ed over the money. Wally handed over his camera (we would both use mine, I told him). We took off our shoes and in we went.

There was hardly anyone else inside, or at least we didn't notice oth-ers. We circled the Sacred Rock and took numerous pictures, from this angle and that, trying to capture through the play of flashlight and shad-ows the cuts and angles on the face of the rock. There still seemed to be no one around.

Now! I said to Wally as, circling, we reached the stairs leading to the cavern below the rock. While Wally stood guard, I rushed down the stairs, my heart palpitating. There were old-time reports of the fate of violators of the Rock's sanctity. Thoughts ran quickly through my mind. Am I violating a taboo, am I right in treading where the Holy of Holies once was, am I right in going where only the High Priest could? But I *am* a Levite, of the priestly tribe! I thought, almost murmuring it to myself. All these thoughts swept over me in a flash, because in no time I was down the steps and inside the cavern. Incredibly, the bottom or under-belly of the Sacred Rock now was roofing over my head!

The place was dimly lit. Light came through the perfectly circular hole bored through the rock, but I wasn't sure (and cannot recall) whether there was another source of light in the cavern. I looked up through the circular opening, and it seemed to have been smoothly cut through: how, by whom, when, and for what purpose remains a mystery. The rest of the rock surface (or bottom) above me did not look like native rock, for I could discern some smooth areas and some niched ones. The same applied to the walls around me, which raised the question whether this cavity was natural or artificially cut.

The floor under my feet was covered with carpets, frustrating my wish to locate an opening farther down. There seemed to be, though, an opening in one side of the cavern, overhung with a cloth curtain. *That's IT!* I thought to myself, recalling a century-old woodcut depicting the place (fig. 157). But as I moved toward it, I almost tripped over seated women, all dressed in black clothing and veiled. They sat motionless and could hardly be discerned in the cavern's dimness, and they literally blocked my way to the opening in the rocky wall.

I had left the camera with Wally, for as curious as I was, I somehow felt that taking pictures with a flashlight in the cavern under the Sacred

Figure 157

Rock was sacrilegious; and I had no flashlight with me to see who was sitting there—if actually women, or perhaps men. For a few moments that felt like eternity, I just stood there, motionless. Then I heard Wally's voice, jarring me to reality. *Quick, someone is coming!* he called out to me. I rushed back up the stairs, in time to be back up when Mahmoud and the heavyset guard approached us. "You must leave!" they said, and we did.

Mahmoud led us to another exit from the Mount, used exclusively by Moslems and leading to the Moslem Quarter. "Better this way," he said, winking.

As I thanked him, he again held on to my extended hand. "Nothing for *me?*" he asked. I pulled out a hundred-shekel bank note. He grimaced as though it was not enough, but took it and thanked me.

As-Sallam—good-bye and peace be with you—I said to him in Arabic, and Wally and I left.

***

That evening, at the briefing session that reviewed the day's eventful experiences, I told the group of what had taken place inside the Dome of the Rock and the cavern under the rock.

Why was it so important to go back there? I was asked. Why was it important to see if there is a cavity or cavern under the cavern, below the Rock?

I explained that the cavern could hold the key to the mystery of the disappearance of the Ark of the Covenant. We know that the Temple built by Solomon was clearly intended to house the Ark of the Covenant, both as a symbol of God's presence and for safekeeping the two Tablets of the Law that represented God's covenant with his Chosen People. Besides serving as the Speaker or speaking device for God's instructions to Moses during the Exodus, it acted as a miraculous device that parted for the Israelites the waters of the Jordan River and caused the walls of Jericho to fall. It was the most important, revered, and sacred object in the Temple, far surpassing in importance all the other utensils, vessels, and man-made ritual objects that were installed in the Temple. And then it disappeared!

Biblical and Egyptian records report that Jerusalem was attacked and plundered by the Pharaoh Sheishak (or Sheshonk) soon after Solomon's death. But neither record (the Egyptian one is on the walls of the Great Temple in Karnak) mentions the Ark among the booty. Some four centuries later, Jerusalem was attacked and sacked by Nebuchadnezzar of

Babylon, but again in the detailed list of plundered objects the Ark is not mentioned. It was not there during the Roman destruction of the Second Temple—the most important and sacred object carried off from the Temple to Rome was the seven-branched candelabra, depicted on the Arch of Titus in Rome (fig. 158). So when and how did the Ark of the Covenant disappear?

When I posed that question to the group, I intended it to be merely rhetorical, but someone in the group spoke up: "They say it was taken to Ethiopia, there is a book about it."

Well, yes, I acknowledged. According to this version, the Queen of Sheba bore a son fathered by King Solomon when she returned to Ethiopia. The son, Menelik, then visited his father in Jerusalem, where he stole the Ark of the Covenant and brought it back with him to Ethiopia. Ethiopian Christian tradition holds that the sacred object has been kept all this time since then at a city called Aksum, in a church inaccessible to all except the church keeper and the high priest. The tale thus alleges a son of Solomon and alleges a hidden site for the Ark, which has never been publicly seen or shown to researchers.

As unlikely as the whole tale appears to be, I observed, it faces two

Figure 158

other problems. One is that Sheba, the Queen's land, is in southern Arabia and not in east Africa. The other is that the Talmud, the record of ancient rabbinical discussions, unmistakably states that the Ark was hidden by King Josiah (641–610 B.C.) as a precaution against the anticipated Babylonian attack. Solomon's alleged son would have been more than four hundred years old by then.

There is a famous Sherlock Holmes mystery, I said, in which the clue to solving the murder was the question, Why did the dog *not* bark? The same question needs to be asked in regard to the disappearance of the most venerated relic of the Exodus and the Ten Commandments: Why wasn't there a hue and cry when the Holy of Holies no longer contained the Ark of the Covenant? When the exiles returned from Babylon to build the Second Temple, the absence of the Ark was taken for granted. It was as if everyone in the know knew that its absence was OK, it was somewhere else safe and sound.

This, I continued, brings us to another version concerning the Ark's departure from the Holy of Holies. This one tells that the Ark was transferred, with priestly consent, to a duplicate temple at a Jewish settlement on the island of Elephantine in Upper Egypt. There are scriptural hints that the Prophet Jeremiah might have been involved in a transfer of the Ark to a safe place abroad; some regard a reference by the Prophet Isaiah to an altar to Yahweh "in the midst of Egypt" as referring to the temple in Elephantine. This version intrigues me, I said, because the island was associated in ancient Egypt with the creator god Khnum, alias Ptah, alias the Sumerian god Enki.

Putting all such versions and speculations aside, I said, one cannot ignore the clearest scriptural statement on the subject. It is the one about the Judean king Josiah. The statement in the Talmud unmistakably says that the Ark was hidden by him *"in its place,"* "under the woods." That suggests that the Ark was not moved from the Temple, but was placed in hiding, "in its place," but "under the woods" in the cavity below the Rock, hidden by a wooden floor!

Therefore, I concluded, to unravel the mystery of the disappeared Ark, one had to examine the cavern and other possible caverns under the Rock in the Holy of Holies.

You did not expect to get down there and find the Ark? I was asked half jokingly. No, I said, but we know from the Bible the measurements of the Ark without the superstructure of the winged cherubim. The Ark proper measured just over four feet by 2.5 by 2.5 feet. So, to be carried out it required at most an opening of just over four feet wide or, if carried sidewise, less than three feet; and that is what I wanted to check—how wide was the first way down (the stairway), and how wide the next opening down (the curtained opening).

And? many shouted out all at once.

As far as I could see, the Ark would have made it through both openings, I said.

So was I suggesting that somewhere, in the next or third cavity down, the Ark of the Covenant is still hidden? The answer, I replied, may lie in the secret gateway in the Western Wall Tunnel and the large cavity behind it. Does it connect to the cavities or caverns under the Sacred Rock? If it does, then the Ark could have been smuggled out away from the Temple Mount; if it doesn't, then the Ark might still be there, in the second cavity.

So the whereabouts of the Ark remains a mystery? some in the group asked.

So it does, I confirmed; but it is not the only mystery. There's still the other mystery, that of the colossal stone blocks. To me there is no question Who Did It; it had to be the Anunnaki. To me there's no question of When—it had to be when the Mount was chosen as the site of the new Mission Control Center, the new DUR.AN.KI. To me the question is Why? Was the Temple Mount platform also a Landing Place, smaller than Baalbek but also needing these massive supports in the Western Wall? Was it meant just to protect an empty cavity, a void space? Or was it built to protect whatever was intended to be behind these blocks, perhaps the instruments that connected Heaven and Earth?

Will we ever know? someone asked.

I hesitated before answering, for I was not sure how to answer this simple question. In the end I said: "One day we will."

✳✳✳

Postscript

After I returned to New York, I recalled my thoughts atop the Temple Mount and its divinely inspiring tranquillity. I looked up in the Bible the verse that had come to my mind that day about God making His appearance in serene silence.

It is found in the tale of the Prophet Elijah, who had to escape from the wrath of Queen Jezebel after her favored priests of the god Ba'al were slain. Escaping southward, he reached Beersheba; then he continued, a day's journey, into the wilderness of the Negev. Tired and hungry, he fell asleep under a juniper tree. "And behold, an Angel appeared and touched him and said: Arise and eat!" And miraculously, there was food and water beside him. With his strength restored, Elijah, on the Angel's instructions, journeyed forty days and forty nights "unto the Mount of the Elohim in Horeb; and he came there unto a cave, and spent the night in it." And the word of the Lord came to him, saying: come out and stand before the Lord!

As Elijah stood outside the cave, awaiting the arrival of his God, there came a strong wind that rent mountains and shattered rocks, "but the Lord was not in the wind." The wind was followed by a quaking of the earth, "but the Lord was not in the earthquake's din." A fire followed, "but the Lord was not in the fire." Then after the fire, "there was a stillness without sound." And God was in the stillness, and His voice addressed Elijah.

I was stunned as I read those verses in the First Book of Kings, chapter 19. When the stillness that engulfed me on the Temple Mount reminded me of the biblical passage asserting that God was in the stillness, I did not recall that it had to do with Elijah's hiding in the cave upon Mount Sinai. Twenty years earlier, in November 1977, I had chartered a plane to find the real Mount Sinai, and my clue was the Elijah Cave. The immediate purpose of that flight was to ascertain the feasibility of the post-Diluvial Landing Corridor, so my flight path began over Jerusalem, over the Temple Mount. Twenty years later—twenty years almost to the day, in September 1997—there I was seized with thoughts upon the Temple Mount itself when an odd stillness engulfed me.

It had to be more than a coincidence.